DK EYEWITNESS TRAVEL

TOP 10
RIO
DE JANEIRO

ALEX ROBINSON

DK | Penguin Random House

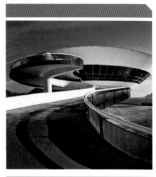

Top 10 Rio de Janeiro Highlights

The Top 10 of Everything

CONTENTS

Rio de Janeiro Area by Area

Streetsmart

Within each Top 10 list in this book, no hierarchy of quality or popularity is implied. All 10 are, in the editor's opinion, of roughly equal merit.
    Throughout this book, floors are referred to in accordance with American usage; i.e., the "first floor" is at ground level.

Front cover and spine *View of Rio de Janeiro from Corcovado to Sugar Loaf Mountain*
Back cover *Tranquil courtyard of a mansion in Parque Lage*
Title page *Sunbathing and kitesurfing on Barra da Tijuca beach*

Welcome to
Rio de Janeiro

Fringed by white-sand beaches, embraced by jungle-clad mountains, and pulsating to the rhythm of *samba*. Carnaval city. Party city. Home to *futebol* – the beautiful game. To the locals, known as *Cariocas*, with their irrepressible love of life, Rio de Janeiro has it all and more. Discover these precious treasures with Eyewitness Top 10 Rio de Janeiro.

We share *Cariocas'* passion for their beloved hometown and Brazil's second city, with its natural wonders of **Pão de Açúcar**, and **Corcovado**, and the endless string of beaches from **Copacabana** to **Barra da Tijuca** and beyond. Then there's the world-famous party at **Carnaval** or the year-round tropical heat best enjoyed by lazing under a palm tree while sipping on a *caipirinha*. **Santa Teresa**'s arty back streets, the verdant splendor of **Jardim Botânico**, and the wildlife-filled **Tijuca National Park** offer more beauty and relaxation.

The city's history, art, and culture are all well preserved within architectural gems, such as the **Mosteiro de São Bento**, or the **Museu Nacional de Belas Artes**, home to one of Latin America's finest art collections.

Rio's entertainment scene is also superb: there are spectacular *samba* shows, sultry *bossanova* and edgy baile funk clubs, and traditional *gafieira* dancehalls. The city's culinary scene doesn't disappoint either, offering everything from gourmet French cuisine and exotic Amazonian delicacies to blowout Brazilian barbecues.

Whether you're coming for a weekend or a whole week, our Top 10 guide is designed to bring together the best of everything the city has to offer. There are tips throughout, from seeking out what's free to avoiding the crowds. The eight easy-to-follow itineraries help you visit a clutch of sights in a short space of time. Add inspiring photography and detailed maps, and you have the essential, pocket-sized travel companion. **Enjoy the book, and enjoy Rio.**

Clockwise from top: **Cristo Redentor, Carnaval performers, the cable car on Sugar Loaf Mountain, café on Copacabana Beach, Escadaria Selarón, Museu de Arte Contemporanea

Exploring Rio de Janeiro

With its dazzling attractions and activities, Rio de Janeiro spoils visitors for choice. Whether you come for a few days or longer, you'll want to make the most of your time in this amazing city. Here are some ideas of how to spend two or four days' sightseeing in Rio de Janeiro.

Ipanema, one of Rio's big beaches, is overlooked by the Dois Irmãos mountain.

Two Days in Rio de Janeiro

Day ❶

MORNING

Take the funicular up to **Corcovado** (see pp12–13); return downtown to visit Rio's historic sights around **Praça XV** (see pp28–9), including **Mosteiro de São Bento** (see pp18–19).

AFTERNOON

Relax on the beach in **Copacabana** (see pp30–1). Stroll along the sea-front Avenida Atlântica and have a drink at one of its street cafés.

Day ❷

MORNING

Go for a hike around **Parque Nacional da Tijuca** (see pp14–15)

before unwinding with a walk under the shady palm trees of the **Jardim Botânico** (see pp24–5).

AFTERNOON

Browse **Ipanema**'s (see pp32–3) trendy boutiques, then ride the cable car up **Sugar Loaf Mountain** (see pp16–17) to watch the sun set over the city. Visit Bohemian **Lapa** (see pp82–5) and go for a dance in a buzzing *samba* club.

0 km 10
0 miles 10

Area of main map

Museu Casa do Pontal
Sítio Burle Marx
TAXI
BIKE
Praia da Barra da Tijuca

Cosme Velho station
COSME VELHO
FUNICULAR
Corcovado

Parque Nacional da Tijuca
LAGOA

Jardim Botânico

Lagoa Rodrigo de Freitas
Fundação Eva Klabin

Ipanema's boutiques
TAXI
Leblon
IPANEMA
Ipanema Beach

Four Days in Rio de Janeiro

Day ❶

MORNING

Take the cable car up Sugar Loaf Mountain *(see pp16–17)* and soak up the panorama below. Tour downtown Centro, starting at **Praça XV** *(see pp28–9)* to visit its historic sights, such as the **Museu Nacional de Belas Artes** *(see pp20–21)*, **Museu Histórico Nacional** *(see pp26–7)*, or the **Mosteiro de São Bento** *(see pp18–19)*.

Cristo Redentor stands atop Corcovado.

AFTERNOON

Have a chilled *agua de coco* (coconut water) on **Ipanema Beach** *(see pp32–3)* then visit the magnificent **Fundação Eva Klabin** *(see p77)* followed by a drink at a bar overlooking Lagoa Rodrigo de Freitas *(see p80)*.

Day ❷

MORNING

Take the first train up to **Corcovado** *(see pp12–13)* and watch the early-morning sun bathe the city below.

AFTERNOON

Explore the cobbled lanes of **Santa Teresa** then hit the streets of **Lapa** *(see pp82–5)*, spending the evening in its vibrant bars and *samba* clubs.

Day ❸

MORNING

Go for a hike around the **Parque Nacional da Tijuca** *(see pp14–15)* and have picnic lunch at one of its *mirantes* (lookout points).

AFTERNOON

Wander the trails of the **Jardim Botânico** *(see pp24–5)* and go for tea at the **Confeitaria Colombo** *(see p67)*. Spend the evening in chic Leblon *(see pp32–3)*.

Day ❹

MORNING

Explore Rio's booming western districts by hiring a bicycle to ride along **Barra da Tijuca**'s *(see p40)* seafront, admiring the surfers taking on its pounding Atlantic breakers.

AFTERNOON

Choose between one of Barra's museums: the lush **Sítio Roberto Burle Marx** *(see p98)* or the quirky **Museu Casa do Pontal** *(see p49)*.

Mosteiro de São Bento
SAÚDE
Praça XV
CENTRO
Museu Nacional de Belas Artes
Museu Histórico Nacional
Cinelândia station
Lapa
Santa Teresa
GLÓRIA
TRAM
CATETE
METRO
Largo do Machado station
TAXI
FLAMENGO
URCA
Sugar Loaf Mountain
Botafogo station
CABLE CAR
BOTAFOGO
TAXI
ardeal Arcoverde station
METRO
LEME
TAXI
Copacabana Beach
Avenida Atlântica
COPACABANA
General Osório station
TAXI
Confeitaria Colombo

0 km   1
0 miles   1

Key
— Two-day Itinerary
— Four-day Itinerary

Top 10 Rio de Janeiro Highlights

Rio de Janeiro's iconic
Cristo Redentor statue

🔟 Rio de Janeiro's Highlights

Rio, like its people, is warm, musical, and devoted to enjoying itself. Each neighborhood has a distinct character, and an unforgettable view of Cristo Redentor, who surveys the city with arms spread in perpetual welcome.

② Parque Nacional da Tijuca

One of the world's largest tracts of urban rain forest, this park has abundant wildlife, waterfalls, and diverse biomes (see pp14–15).

① Corcovado

The Christ statue was voted one of the seven wonders of the modern world. Views from here are wonderful (see pp12–13).

③ Sugar Loaf Mountain

This boulder-shaped mountain at the south end of Botafogo beach boasts magnificent views. The summit is reached by cable car (see pp16–17).

COSME VELHO

LAGOA

R. JARDIM BOTÂNICO

AVENIDA BORGES DE MEDEIROS

Lagoa Rodrigo de Freitas

AV EPITÁCIO PESSOA

AV. VISCONDE DE ALBUQUERQUE

AV AFRANIO DE MELO FRANCO

LEBLON

IPANEMA

AV VIEIRA SOUTO

Praia do Leblon

Praia de Ipanema

④ Mosteiro de São Bento

This Benedictine church and abbey was founded in 1590, although most of its gilt interior dates from the 1600s (see pp18–19).

Museu Nacional de Belas Artes ⑤

The country's first art gallery displays Brazilian art from colonial times to the late 20th century, as well as works by international masters such as Rodin (see pp20–1).

Jardim Botânico
6
Rio's botanical gardens, founded in 1808 by Prince Regent João, preserve nearly 8,000 species of plants. The orchids are particularly notable *(see pp24–5)*.

Museu Histórico Nacional
7
This museum explores Brazilian history from prehistoric times, with replica rock paintings from the Serra da Capivara, through to the early days of the republic *(see pp26–7)*.

Praça XV
8
This square has the city's largest concentration of pre-20th-century buildings *(see pp28–9)*.

Praia de Copacabana
9
One of the world's most famous urban beaches stretches for 2.5 miles (4 km) from the Morro do Leme, at the northern end, to Arpoador in the south. This tourist hub is renowned for its New Year celebrations *(see pp30–1)*.

Ipanema and Leblon Beachlife
10
Rio's most desirable beaches, just south of Copacabana, front fashionable neighbor-hoods, which are a magnet for tourists *(see pp32–3)*.

🔟 ⭐ Corcovado

The iconic Cristo Redentor (Christ the Redeemer) watches over Rio de Janeiro from the 2,316-ft (706-m) high Corcovado, named for the Portuguese word for hunchback. The winning design in a competition for a monument to represent the spirit of the city, it was inaugurated in 1931 and has come to symbolize Brazil. The journey to Christ's feet – through the streets of Cosme Velho and the Parque Nacional da Tijuca *(see pp14–15)* – is as rewarding as the panorama from the summit.

Cristo Redentor ①

Embracing the city with open arms, the magnificent 98-ft (30-m) tall statue of Jesus Christ **(right)** was designed by Brazilian Heitor da Silva Costa, and draws inspiration from Leonardo da Vinci's famous study of the human body. The structure was hauled up the mountain in pieces and took years to assemble.

② Art Deco Features

The figure was carved from blocks of soapstone **(left)** by French Art Deco sculptor Paul Landowski, known for his Art Deco statue of St. Geneviève in Paris.

③ The Chapel at the Base of the Statue

Underneath the figure, facing away from the sea, this small chapel is a haven of peace amid the tourist crowds. Mass is held here daily at 11am.

④ Refreshments

The bars and restaurants behind and below the statue offer cold drinks, light meals, and welcome shade from the sun **(below)**.

⑤ The Forest Setting

Corcovado is surrounded by the Parque Nacional da Tijuca. The views across the canopy are beautiful in the late afternoon when the setting sun burns a deep orange behind the trees.

⑥ Sunsets and Sunrises

For the classic view of Rio **(above)**, come early in the morning or late in the day when the light is soft and the sun either rises from the bay or sets behind the Floresta da Tijuca *(see p14)*.

7 The Trem do Corcovado

The funicular railway **(below)** runs from Cosme Velho to the summit. Opened in 1884, it is 47 years older than the Christ statue.

A SEVENTH WONDER

In 2007 Rio's Cristo Redentor was declared one of the winners in a worldwide poll to find the "New Seven Wonders of the World" – a modern version of Greek historian Herodotus' list from the 5th century BC. The New Open World Corporation poll is thought to have been the largest ever, with 100 million voters.

8 The Trem do Corcovado Museum

This museum **(left)** explores the history of the railway and the Christ statue. On display are the original 19th-century carriage and engine.

9 Lookout Points

There are panoramic views out over the city and Guanabara Bay from the platform at Christ's feet. The platforms behind and below the statue offer fine views of Parque Nacional da Tijuca.

10 Helicopter Tours

Flights by helicopter offer breathtaking views of the statue and Corcovado. The early morning provides the best light to enhance the experience.

NEED TO KNOW

MAP M1 ■ Rua Cosme Velho 513, Corcovado ■ (21) 2558 1329 ■ www.corcovado.com.br

Open 8:30am–7pm daily

Funicular railway (Trem do Corcovado): US$22; organized tour: US$8; or taxi till Estrada das Paineiras and an authorized van thereafter; you cannot drive up in your own vehicle

■ Do not walk back from Corcovado after dark. Muggings are common on the park road and the street lighting is poor.

■ Cafés are expensive so bring water.

🔟 ⭐ Parque Nacional da Tijuca

This stunning national park contains the Floresta da Tijuca (Tijuca Forest), one of the world's largest urban forests. It also features the dramatic Serra de Carioca (Carioca Mountains), the impressive Pedra da Gávea monolith, and Cristo Redentor, which looms over the city from the top of Corcovado (see pp12–13). Home to countless species of plants and animals, as well as waterfalls and springs, this peaceful forest, which covers 15 sq miles (39 sq km), is a little piece of paradise.

1 Os Esquilos
A favorite lunch spot on Sundays for wealthy Cariocas, Os Esquilos or "Squirrels" restaurant, is romantically situated under the shade of trees in the heart of this park.

3 Trails and Walks
Many trails cut through Floresta da Tijuca, the lengths of which can vary greatly. There are full-day hikes to the park's peaks, at Pedra da Gávea and Pico da Tijuca.

Floresta da Tijuca

2 Hang-Gliding
A very popular hang-gliding spot **(above)**, the Pedra Bonita (another monolith) is next to Pedra da Gávea and is accessible by road and a short trail. Flights can be fixed through tour operators (see p42).

4 Cascatinha do Taunay
The most accessible of the numerous waterfalls that lie in Floresta da Tijuca can be found just off the road a few miles from the Alto da Boa Vista park gate **(left)**. Its spectacular cascades plummet from a height of 100 ft (30 m).

5 Wildlife
The endemic wildlife in Parque Nacional da Tijuca includes primates such as the tiny tufted-eared marmoset **(above)**, as well as 200 species of birds, many of which are critically endangered.

6 Park Roads

A series of roads **(left)** run through the park, connecting the neighborhoods of Santa Teresa, Jardim Botânico, and Barra da Tijuca. Route maps are available in the visitors' center.

REFORESTATION IN IMPERIAL RIO

Deforestation of Tijuca to make room for sugar and coffee plantations during the early years of colonial rule led to such bad flooding that Emperor Dom Pedro II commissioned its reforestation in 1861. It took 13 years for army major Manuel Gomes Archer and six unnamed African slaves to re-plant the forest with native and exotic trees.

9 The Mayrink Chapel

The panels inside this tiny 1863 chapel are replicas of paintings by the Brazilian Modernist artist Cândido Portinari. The originals are in the Museu Nacional de Belas Artes *(see pp20–21)*.

10 Mirante Andaime Pequeno

This is another fantastic lookout point, which looms over the Jardim Botânico neighborhood. It offers sweeping vistas across emerald-green treetops to the striking Corcovado mountain and Cristo Redentor.

NEED TO KNOW

MAP D4 ▪ *Visitors' center:* Praça Afonso Viseu, Alto da Boa Vista: (21) 2492 2253; open 8am–5pm daily ▪ *Os Esquilos:* Estrada Barão D'Escragnole, Alto da Boa Vista, Tijuca; (21) 2492 2197 (cash only)

For tours with Rio Hiking visit www. riohiking.com.br

▪ Winding trails and few signposts make it easy to get lost, so it is best either to come on a tour or hire a guide.

▪ Bring water and a snack; there are few restaurants in the park.

7 Pedra da Gávea

Said to be the world's largest coastal monolith, this granite boulder on the forest's edge over-looks Rio's suburbs.

8 Mirante Dona Marta

This lookout **(above)**, which is perched above the beachfront neighborhood of Botafogo, boasts breathtaking views of the Sugar Loaf *(see pp16–17)*. Note that this area is not safe to visit after dark.

★ Sugar Loaf Mountain

None of Rio's magnificent views are more breathtaking than those from the top of the 1,312-ft (400-m) high granite and quartz Pão de Açúcar (Sugar Loaf) at the mouth of Guanabara Bay. Marmosets, tanagers, and myriad birds are a common sight on the trails that run around the monolith's summit. Visit early in the day or after rain for the clearest views from here and its majestic neighbor – Morro da Urca.

3 Morro da Urca
From Corcovado, the Sugar Loaf resembles a sphinx **(left)**, whose body is made up of Morro da Urca – a separate, lower boulder mountain with a flat summit.

4 Bars and Cafés
Set in the shade of trees, bars and cafés around the Sugar Loaf offer refreshment and respite from the sun.

5 Helicopter Tours
Flights **(right)** out over the iconic triumvirate of Sugar Loaf, Corcovado, and the massive Estádio do Maracanã leave from Morro da Urca and Lagoa Rodrigo de Freitas (see p76), which lies just to the north of Ipanema.

1 Rock Climbing
Tour agencies offer rock-climbing trips (see p43) suitable for both experienced and novice climbers. Rio's stunning views make not looking down a challenge.

2 The Path Up Morro da Urca
The Pista Cláudio Coutinho starts from the suburb of Urca, next to Praia Vermelha, and connects to a trail up to the summit of Morro da Urca. Allow at least one hour for the walk and take plenty of water with you (see p73).

6 Walks at the Summit
Winding trails meander around the summit of the Sugar Loaf. Walks lead through shady forests abundant with tropical birds and butterflies, and lead to a multitude of lookout points that offer views across the city **(left)**.

7 The Sugar Loaf

The Sugar Loaf **(below)** is one of the highest points above sea level in Rio de Janeiro and is reachable by cable car from Morro da Urca. The first recorded solo climb of the Sugar Loaf was made by British nanny Henrietta Carstairs in 1817.

10 The Cable Car

The cable car **(above)** runs from the suburb of Urca to the summit of the Sugar Loaf via Morro da Urca, making it accessible to people of all levels of fitness. Those looking for a hike can also walk up to the summit.

PÃO DE AÇÚCAR

The name of Sugar Loaf, adopted in the 19th century, is derived from the rock's shape, which resembles the conical clay molds once used to refine sugar. The indigenous Tupi Guarani people, however, called it *Pau-nh-acqua* (high, pointed, or isolated hill).

8 Views of the City

There is a dramatic, 360-degree view out over Rio, Guanabara Bay, and the surrounding rain forest-covered mountains from a variety of lookout points located on both Morro da Urca and Sugar Loaf Mountain **(below)**.

9 Wildlife

Tufted-eared marmosets and various species of rare birds, including the seven-colored tanager, are a common sight on the Sugar Loaf. The trees are adorned with bromeliads, orchids, and other flora.

NEED TO KNOW

MAP J4 ■ Av Pasteur 520, Urca ■ (21) 2546 8400 ■ Cable cars leave from Urca every 20 minutes

Open 8am–7:50pm ■ Adm US$26

■ Allow at least three hours to see both the Sugar Loaf and Morro da Urca.

■ There are cafés on both hills, and drinks and snacks are available from the cable car station in Urca.

TOP 10 ⭐ Mosteiro de São Bento

The Benedictines, the first religious order to establish itself firmly in Brazil, founded this magnificent hilltop monastery and church in 1590. Dedicated to Our Lady of Montserrat, one of the black Madonnas of Europe, it boasts richly decorated interiors that date from the 18th century – the formative years of Brazilian Baroque. The interior took almost 70 years to complete and was the life work of a series of artists, notably Benedictine monk Frei Domingos da Conceição (1643–1718).

1 Facade
The unadorned, sober facade of the monastery **(right)**, with its whitewashed plaster, raw stone masonry, and squat geometrical towers, contrasts starkly with the gilded opulence of the interior.

3 Baroque Doors
The elaborately carved Baroque doors that provide access to the nave are also considered to be the work of Frei Domingos da Conceição. They are thought to have been carved in the period between 1699 and the monk's death in 1718.

4 Candelabras
The church was originally illuminated by candles held in ornate candelabras cast from silver by the artist Mestre Valentim. The most impressive of these still sit next to the altarpiece.

2 Statue of St. Scholastica
A glorious work by sculptor Frei Domingos da Conceição, this intricately carved statue **(above)** depicts St. Scholastica, who was the twin sister of St. Benedict. The saint's name stands for "she who is devoted to theological study."

5 Paintings by Frei Ricardo Pilar
The painting *Christ of the Martyrs* by the German Benedictine monk Ricardo Pilar dates from 1690 and is the finest of all his paintings on display in the church.

NEED TO KNOW

MAP W1 ▪ Rua Dom Gerardo 68, Centro (entrance by elevator at No. 40) ▪ (21) 2206 8100 ▪ www.osb.org.br

Open 7am–5:30pm daily

▪ Photography of any kind is not permitted in the church.

▪ There are no drinks available at the monastery, so be sure to carry water.

6 Chapel of the Santíssimo

This chapel is the most sacred part of the church. It preserves the consecrated host – bread that Catholics believe to be the body of Christ – and has lavish Rococo features, such as the gilded carvings and a burnished sacred heart **(left)**.

ST. BENEDICT

St. Benedict of Nursia, the founder of Western monasticism, was a Roman noble who fled the city to live as a hermit. Inspired by his saintliness, the community of a nearby abbey requested St. Benedict to be their leader. He later founded a monastery, where he wrote the Rule of the Benedictine Order.

9 The Library

The monastery's library **(below)** preserves one of the finest collections of ancient religious books in Brazil. It is open only to those members of the public who have requested permission in writing from the abbot.

7 Statue of St. Benedict

Regarded as one of the crowning achievements of Baroque in Rio de Janeiro, this elaborate statue of the founder of the Benedictine order forms a part of the altarpiece, which is located at the back of the church **(above)**.

10 Statue of Our Lady of Montserrat

This statue of the patron saint of the church was also created by Frei Domingos da Conceição. There are many other paintings of the patron saint adorning the walls of the church and monastery.

8 Gilded Ornamentation

The Brazilian Baroque interior of the church is considered the most ornate in Rio, with almost every square inch richly decorated with gold leaf **(left)**.

🔟 ⭐ Museu Nacional de Belas Artes

Housing the most comprehensive collection of Brazilian art in the country, the National Museum of Fine Arts was established in 1937 in the former Brazilian Academy of Fine Arts building. The collection comprises close to 20,000 pieces, including fine, decorative, and popular art. The majority of works are Brazilian from the 17th to the 20th centuries. A small number are foreign, predominantly from Europe.

3 The Sculpture Gallery

A corridor lined with statues looking out on to a central space, this gallery **(right)** houses works that include classical reproductions and original pieces by artists such as Rodin and Brecheret.

1 Almeida's Arrufos

Avant-garde painter Belmiro de Almeida learned cutting-edge styles in Europe in the 1880s. *Arrufos* **(above)**, painted in 1887, is considered his masterpiece.

4 Portadora de Perfumes

Victor Brecheret, Brazil's most highly respected sculptor, was one of Latin America's foremost practitioners of Art Deco. His work can be seen across Brazil. *Portadora de Perfumes* was cast from bronze in 1923.

5 Batalha do Avaí

Brazilian painter Pedro Américo's epic work, a majestic mock-European canvas, depicts the decisive battle of the 1868 war between Paraguay and the triple alliance of Uruguay, Argentina, and Brazil.

6 Pernambuco Landscapes

Some of the earliest Brazilian landscapes were painted in the 17th century by expatriate artists in Dutch-occupied Pernambuco. The most famous of these artists was Franz Post.

2 Primeira Missa no Brasil

Victor Meirelles's 1861 painting **(above)**, fully restored in 2007, depicts the moment the Portuguese first recited mass on Brazilian soil.

7 Works by Tarsila do Amaral

Do Amaral and her husband, Oswald de Andrade, defined the first distinctly Brazilian approach to art, which they termed *antropofagismo*. This involved adapting Western themes to Brazilian contexts **(left)**.

THE FRENCH CULTURAL MISSION

When the Portuguese royal family arrived in Rio in 1808, they were determined to turn it into a European-style city. In 1816 they invited the Frenchman Joaquim Le Breton to head a cultural mission to establish European high culture in the city. One of his first endeavors was to establish the Academy of Fine Arts.

9 European Engravings

One of the museum's collections preserves an important archive of engravings and sketches by a number of famous European painters and illustrators including Goya, Doré, and Picasso.

10 Café by Portinari

Cândido Portinari, a graduate of Rio's Escola Nacional de Belas Artes, was one of Brazil's most influential Modernist painters. His work falls into two periods: *Café* **(below)** is an example of Social Realism and draws inspiration from Mexican muralists such as Diego Rivera, while most of his other work is Expressionistic.

NEED TO KNOW

MAP X3 ■ Av Rio Branco 199, Centro
■ (21) 2219 8474
■ www.mnba.gov.br

Open 10am–6pm Tue–Fri, noon–5pm Sat, Sun & hols

Admission: US$2.50 (free on Sun)

■ Visit in the middle of the day when Rio is at its hottest and the gallery is less busy.

■ The Teatro Municipal, across Avenida Rio Branco in Cinelândia, has an excellent café *(see p69)*.

8 Rodin's Meditação Sem Braço

The Modernist sculptor's tortured *Meditação Sem Braço* (Meditation without Arms) was acquired by Fundação Roberto Marinho.

Following pages The statue of Cristo Redentor gazes out over the city and bay

TOP 10 ⭐ Jardim Botânico

Tucked away behind Lagoa Rodrigo de Freitas and Ipanema beach, Rio's shady Jardim Botânico offers a haven from the urban rush. Founded by Prince Regent João in 1808 as a repository for imported plants to become acclimatized to the tropics, the gardens were opened to the public after the Proclamation of the Republic in 1889. Plants are grouped in distinct areas linked by gravel paths and interspersed with streams and waterfalls. The gardens lend their name to the neighborhood, which has excellent restaurants and nightlife.

1 Views of Corcovado

The gardens boast wonderful views of Corcovado (see pp12–13), which is visible in the distance through the trees. The ideal time for taking photographs is in the late afternoon, when visitors start to leave and the light is at its best.

2 The Avenue of Palms

The stately Avenue of Palms **(above)** is located in the center of the gardens close to a magnificent classical fountain. It is lined with 40-ft (13-m) tall palms, which were planted at the time the gardens were established.

3 The Arboretum

The garden is home to some 8,000 plant species, including the many native Brazilian trees in the arboretum.

4 Fountains

These lush gardens are relatively quiet, except for the soothing tinkle of running water from the elaborate 19th-century fountains that pepper the grounds **(right)**. This, and the incessant birdsong, offers a welcome break from the noisy streets.

6 Museu Casa dos Pilões

This simple, whitewashed cottage **(left)**, hidden away near the Orquidarium, was once the center for grinding saltpeter, charcoal, and sulfur into gunpowder for the 1808 Royal Rio de Janeiro Gunpowder Factory, which is also in the garden.

5 The Café Botânico

Cariocas visit Jardim Botânico not just to enjoy the stunningly diverse plant life, but also to enjoy a coffee or light lunch in the open-air café, next to the cactus gardens.

7 The Orquidarium

This part of the garden is home to some of the world's most rare orchids, including the famous *Cattleya* **(below)**. Some 1,000 tropical orchids are cultivated and preserved here.

8 Giant Amazon Lilies

The world's largest waterlilies **(left)**, the *Victoria amazonica* or *Victoria regia* are cultivated on ponds in the gardens. Discovered in the 19th century, the lily was named for British monarch Queen Victoria.

A BOTANICAL ARK

Brazil has more than 21 million hectares (52 million acres) of nature preserves, which amounts to less than 2 percent of the country's territory. According to botanists, this is far too little to ensure the preservation of many vulnerable natural habitats. Botanical gardens play a crucial role in plant conservation, preserving many rare species.

NEED TO KNOW

MAP L3 ▪ Rua Jardim Botânico 1008 ▪ (21) 3874 1808 ▪ www.jbrj. gov.br ▪ Bus 170 from the center, 573 from Glória and Lapa, or 570 from Copacabana and Ipanema

Open 8am–5pm Tue– Sun, noon–5pm Mon

Admission: US$4.50

▪ The best time to see birds and marmosets is in the early morning during the week, when visitor numbers are low.

9 Bird-Watching

The gardens offer some of the best urban bird-watching in Brazil **(above)**. Woodnymphs, foliage-gleaners, thrushes, parakeets, woodcreepers, and aplomado falcons are the easiest to spot.

10 The Jardim dos Beija-Flores

This beautiful hummingbird garden has been planted with hundreds of brightly colored flowering plants that attract butterflies, such as the Blue Morpho, as well as more than 20 different species of hummingbird.

TOP 10 ★ Museu Histórico Nacional

Rio's most interesting museum is devoted to the human history of Brazil. Exhibits include paintings, sculptures, photographs, maps, and other historical artifacts. Galleries are dedicated to Brazil's indigenous tribes, while the colonial, imperial, and republican eras are also well represented. Visitors can see a replica of the prehistoric rock paintings from the Serra da Capivara in the northeast of Brazil, claimed to be the oldest record of human presence in South America.

5 Statue of Dom Pedro II
This romanticized statue by a Carioca sculptor was first exhibited at the 1867 Paris Exhibition and portrays Emperor Dom Pedro II riding a horse.

1 Citizenship in Construction
Focusing on political, civil, and social rights from 1889 to the present, this exhibition **(above)** displays paintings of leading historical figures and events, as well as videos of 20th-century life in Brazil.

2 Portuguese Around the World
This area of the museum covers 400 years of history, from the Portuguese colonization of Brazil, through the gold and diamond booms, to the 1822 Proclamation of Independence.

3 Imperial Thrones
The thrones displayed at the museum **(right)** were the seats of state, used for grand occasions by the Portuguese exiled king, João VI, and by the Brazilian Emperors Dom Pedro I and Pedro II.

4 Constitution of the Nation
These galleries chart Brazil's path to independence: the War of the Triple Alliance, the abolition of slavery, and the social uprising leading to the exile of the Portuguese royal family, and the 1889 Proclamation of the Republic.

NEED TO KNOW

MAP Y3 ■ Praça Marechal Âncora, Centro ■ (21) 2550 9224 ■ Adm US$4 (free on Sun) ■ www.museu historiconacional.com.br

Open 10am–5:30pm Tue–Fri, 2–6pm Sat–Sun

■ The museum can be visited on the way to or from Praça XV *(see pp28–9)*.

■ Set aside three hours or more to explore the museum fully.

■ The museum has an excellent café on the first floor.

⑧ Farmácia Teixeira Novaes

A full-scale, mood-lit reproduction of an 18th-century Rio de Janeiro apothecary shop **(left)**, this exhibit also includes a replica of the back office and laboratory.

THE BUILDING

The museum is housed in a former arsenal and retains a wall from the city's first fort – a reminder of Rio's colonial past. The city center was once as grand as that of Buenos Aires, but the hill, the fort, and much of Portuguese Rio were demolished post independence in order to break away from its colonial history.

⑨ Pátio dos Canhões

This atrium is filled with rusting cannons, many of which date to the colonial period. Others come from the UK and France.

⑥ Royal Carriages

As the only South American country to have had a monarchy, Brazil retains many vestiges of its royal past. The museum houses the carriages of both Emperor Dom Pedro II and Empress Teresa Christina **(above)**.

⑦ Temporary Galleries

Some of Rio's most exciting visiting shows are displayed here. Information about the exhibitions can be found on the museum website.

Key to Floorplan

1st floor
2nd floor

⑩ Combate Naval do Riachuelo

Victor Meirelles' grand and sweeping canvas, in the spirit of the European Romantics, idealizes the Brazilian campaign against Paraguay in the War of the Triple Alliance – the only war that Brazil has fought.

🔟⭐ Praça XV

Praça XV was the first area to develop during the 18th century Minas Gerais gold rush, which transformed Rio from a scruffy port town into a wealthy city. The square became a trading center, and trade still takes place here in the market next to Rua 1 de Março. It also served as the center of Brazil's political power under the Portuguese. Today, Praça XV is dotted with historical buildings and streets. The 1980s restoration of the Paço Imperial catalyzed the return of culture to the city center.

1 Exhibition Galleries
Today, the Paço Imperial serves as a cultural center, hosting some of Rio's best small exhibitions, many devoted to the nation's history and cultural life.

2 Igreja Santa Cruz dos Militares
This was one of Rio de Janeiro's grandest churches when it was built in the 17th century. Badly damaged in a fire in 1923, it was restored and still retains a few original details attributed to the celebrated sculptor Mestre Valentim, who created its carvings (below).

3 Estação das Barcas
With its prominent clock and faux-Baroque architecture, this boat station (above) was the hub of Brazil's international trade – most of which came through Rio.

4 Palácio Tiradentes
This 1920s palace is the seat of the Legislative Assembly of the State of Rio de Janeiro. A statue of Tiradentes – the first Brazilian to rebel against the Portuguese – stands in front of the building.

5 Igreja de Nossa Senhora do Carmo da Antiga Sé
Known as the Old Cathedral, this church's modest exterior encloses a beautiful interior with a Rococo nave, ceiling panels, and wall carvings.

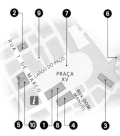

6 Ferry Dock
The Portuguese royal family disembarked just to the west of this spot when they arrived here in 1808. Today, ferries leave from the dock for Niterói, across the bay.

7 Chafariz do Mestre Valentim

This public drinking fountain **(left)** was designed in 1789 by Mestre Valentim, one of the city's most important Baroque artists. It was intended for use by sailors whose boats were moored on the nearby quays.

MAD QUEEN MARIA

The Faculdade Cândido Mendes at Praça XV 101, formerly a Carmelite convent, was used to incarcerate Portugal's Queen Maria, whose mood oscillated between religious fervor and depression. Her son, João (later King João VI), ruled in her stead as Regent until her death in 1816.

10 Igreja da Ordem Terceira de Nossa Senhora do Monte do Carmo

Situated next to the Old Cathedral, this 18th-century church boasts an opulent interior covered in gilt carvings **(left)**, many by Mestre Valentim.

NEED TO KNOW

MAP X2

Igreja Santa Cruz dos Militares: Rua 1 de Março 36

Paço Imperial and Exhibition Galleries: Praça XV 48. **Open** noon–6pm Tue–Sun

Palácio Tiradentes: Rua Primeiro de Março s/n. **Open** 10am–5pm Mon–Sat, noon–5pm Sun & hols

Igreja de Nossa Senhora do Carmo da Antiga Sé: Rua 1 de Março. **Open** 8:30am–3:30pm Mon–Fri, 10am–noon Sat, 9am & 11am Sun (for masses)

Igreja da Ordem Terceira de Nossa Senhora do Monte do Carmo: Rua Primeiro de Março s/n. **Open** 8am–4pm Mon–Fri, 8–11am Sat

■ Avoid the empty square at weekends.

8 Paço Imperial

This modest colonial building was built in 1743 as the seat of government. When the Portuguese royal family arrived in Brazil in 1808, a third floor was added and the building became the Imperial Palace.

9 Travessa do Comércio

This charming pedestrian street is lined with bars and restaurants **(left)**. Carmen Miranda lived in a house in this alley as a young girl.

🔟 ⭐ Praia de Copacabana

One of Rio's most celebrated beaches, Copacabana stretches from the Morro do Leme in the northeast to the Arpoador in the southwest. It is a year-round tourist hub, famed for its New Year's Eve celebrations. When a tunnel connected the area with Botafogo in 1892, Copacabana was an unspoilt bay with picturesque dunes. By the time the Copacabana Palace was built, the neighborhood had more than 30,000 residents. Today, it is one of the most densely populated areas in the world.

1 Forte Duque de Caxias

This 18th-century fort is also called Forte do Leme. A steep climb from the beach, it is named for the general who fought in the 1868 War of the Triple Alliance. The views are spectacular **(left)**.

2 Copacabana Palace

Many famous visitors have stayed at this grand Art Deco hotel. Pictures of past celebrity guests are displayed on the second floor *(see p112)*.

3 New Year's Eve

Copacabana hosts Rio's biggest New Year's Eve party, when as many as 2 million people gather to listen to live music concerts and watch the midnight fireworks.

4 Mosaic Pavements

Copacabana's unique black-and-white wave-patterned pavements form a beachfront promenade that is typically Portuguese in style. They were designed by Brazilian landscape architect Roberto Burle Marx.

5 Beach Soccer

The beach, which is several times wider than a soccer field is long, is the place where *favela* kids have long honed their soccer skills.

6 Forte de Copacabana

This fort at the southern end **(below)** affords great views along the beach. A museum here charts the history of the army in Brazil from colonial times.

NEED TO KNOW
MAP Q5–R3

■ The beach is well floodlit all night, but it is best avoided after dark as criminals often target the area.

■ On Sundays, the road closest to the beach is closed to traffic, so this is a particularly good day for cycling and jogging along the beachside track that leads west all the way to Barra da Tijuca.

■ There are bicycle hire stands along the beach.

■ The beach is lined with numerous cafés and stalls selling cold, fresh coconut water.

9 Morro do Leme

Copacabana is marked by a monolith – the Morro do Leme **(above)** – which is partially covered with forest. Take the trails up the hill at weekends when guards monitor the entrance.

7 Copacabana and Leme Neighborhoods

Copacabana beach fronts two neighborhoods – Leme and Copacabana itself. The area is filled with hotels, and vibrant restaurants, bars, and shops **(above)**.

8 Beach Vendors

Beer, snacks like the *biscoito globo*, sun umbrellas, *cangas*, flip-flops, and massages are all offered by itinerant beach vendors, who walk along the beach from dawn to dusk proffering their wares.

10 Fishermen

In the late 19th century, southern Copacabana was home only to a fort and a tiny fishing community, whose descendants own the colorful fishing boats **(above)** that sit on the sand next to Forte de Copacabana.

TOP 10 ⭐ Ipanema and Leblon Beachlife

Ipanema and its extension farther south, Leblon, are urban Rio's most beautiful, fashionable, and secure beaches. Most tourists make their base at the two wealthy neighborhoods located behind their eponymous beaches where chic boutiques and glamorous restaurants line the streets. Neighboring Copacabana, the Jardim Botânico, Gávea, and Corcovada, are easily reached from here.

1 Cycling and Running Tracks

For health-conscious visitors looking for more than sunbathing and lounging on the sand, there are 2-mile- (3.5-km-) long cycling and running tracks **(right)** along the entire length of both beaches.

2 Beach Exercise

Alongside a multitude of home-grown beach sports, exercising on the sand in these body-conscious neighborhoods is a vanity fair. A popular spot for this is around the pull-up bars in front of Rua Farme de Amoedo, which is the posing ground for the most tanned and toned.

3 Farme Beach

This stretch, between Postos 8 and 9, is the favorite daytime haunt for Rio's gay and lesbian community. Look for the rainbow flags, displayed with pride by beach vendors **(below)**.

4 Beach Volleyball and Footvolley

Brazilians are the best in the world at beach volleyball and the national women's team practice on Ipanema. Footvolley is played entirely with the feet and head *(see p45)*.

5 Beachwear

The essential Ipanema and Leblon beach kit comprises a *tanga* and *canga* (bikini and sarong) and sunglasses for women, and a *sunga* and *havaianas* (speedos and flip-flops) for men. You can buy these items from the vendors behind the beach *(see p54)*.

6 Children's Play Areas

There are kids' play areas **(above)** at the Baixo Bebê kiosk *(see p48)* on Leblon beach and in Praça Nossa Senhora da Paz, behind Ipanema beach.

THE GIRL FROM IPANEMA

Poet Vinícius de Moraes and composer Antônio Carlos Jobim wrote *The Girl from Ipanema* in homage to a beautiful teenager called Heloisa Pinheiro who, on her way to the beach, used to pass the café where the men would meet for an afternoon beer.

8 Beachside Cafés

The beachside kiosks that line Ipanema and Leblon beaches serve snacks, drinks, and delicious ice-cold coconut water, drunk straight from the coconut shell. The cafés also offer shade from the sun.

Cariocas relax in the sun on Ipanema Beach

9 Sand Sculptures

Carioca artists create elaborate fantasy castles and sculptures from Ipanema's fine sand **(above)**. Look out for them right next to the running tracks.

NEED TO KNOW

MAP M6–N6 *Ipanema*

MAP L6 *Leblon*

■ Avoid walking on the beach after dark.

■ Energy drinks can be bought from juice bars throughout Ipanema and Leblon.

7 Postos

These concrete bunkers on the beach are more than lifeguard stations – social status is reflected by the location of your towel on the beach. The closer you are to the most fashion-able position, near Posto Nove (9) in Ipanema, the higher your status.

10 Beach Massage

Massages on makeshift couches and chairs have been available on Ipanema and Leblon for decades, and tend to be of a very high standard and reasonably priced.

The Top 10 of Everything

Oscar Niemeyer's stunning Museu de
Arte Contemporanea de Niterói

🔟 Moments in History

Engraving of the Proclamation of the Republic of Brazil on November 15, 1889

1 The First Brazilians

Brazil's first inhabitants are believed to have traveled across temporary land bridges that connected Asia and America at the Bering Straits. They then traveled south through the Americas between 40,000 and 12,000 years ago.

2 Portuguese Land in Rio

On January 1, 1502, the Portuguese explorer Gaspar de Lemos arrived in Guanabara Bay – which he mistakenly named Rio de Janeiro (January River) – and he built a small fort to claim the bay for Portugal. But hostile confrontations with the indigenous Tamoio people led the Portuguese to establish their colony elsewhere in Brazil.

3 The French Arrive

In 1555, France sent a fleet of ships under Admiral Nicolas Durand de Villegagnon to Rio, where they claimed a tiny island in Guanabara Bay. The French treated the Tamoios far better than the Portuguese had done and succeeded in forging a military alliance with them.

4 The Portuguese Defeat the French–Tamoio Alliance

The Portuguese returned to Rio and, with various indigenous groups, fought numerous battles against the French–Tamoio Alliance, eventually defeating it on January 20, 1567.

5 The Portuguese Royal Court Moves to Rio

In November 1807, the entire Portuguese royal family fled Napoleon. Their fleet comprised some 40 ships packed with 15,000 members of the Portuguese court and government, and Rio became the capital of Portugal.

Emperor Dom Pedro I

6 The French Cultural Mission

In 1816, King Dom João VI of Portugal invited the French to introduce European culture to Rio by bringing in their styles of architecture, art, and music (see p21).

7 Pedro I Declares Independence

King Dom João VI returned to Portugal in 1821, leaving his son

Pedro as Prince Regent in Brazil. Pedro declared independence from Portugal the next year, and crowned himself Emperor Dom Pedro I. He and his son, Pedro II, ruled over the new country for the next 67 years.

⑧ Brazil Becomes a Republic

The republican movement of 1870 was provoked by general discontent over high taxes and the movement toward the abolition of slavery. On November 15, 1889, Emperor Dom Pedro II was overthrown and the republic was proclaimed by Marechal Deodoro da Fonseca.

⑨ The Capital Moves from Rio to Brasilia

Rio de Janeiro was replaced by Brasilia as capital of Brazil in 1960. This change was overseen by President Juscelino Kubitschek and three Modernist architects, Lúcio Costa, Oscar Niemeyer (see p72), and Roberto Burle Marx.

⑩ Rio Hosts the World Environmental Summit

On June 3, 1992, Rio hosted the Earth Summit – the first and largest global conference of its kind on the environment. It provided an impetus for Brazil to review its own environmental record and change the way the national economy was run.

Emperor Dom Pedro II

TOP 10 HISTORICAL FIGURES

Chief Cunhambebe

1 Chief Cunhambebe
The ferocious giant chief of the Tamoios, who almost defeated the Portuguese.

2 Gaspar de Lemos
The first European to see Rio was also present when Álvares Cabral "discovered" Brazil in 1500.

3 Nicholas de Villegagnon
The Frenchman responsible for claiming an island in Guanabara Bay and forging alliances with the Tamoios.

4 Mem de Sá
One of Portugal's most ruthless and effective generals, Mem de Sá founded Rio along with his 17-year-old nephew, Estácio, in 1565.

5 João VI of Portugal
This Regent fled Portugal in 1808, founded imperial Brazil, and later became King João VI.

6 Emperor Dom Pedro I
Son of João VI, declarer of independence, and the first emperor of free Brazil.

7 Emperor Dom Pedro II
Pedro I's son, who helped abolish slavery and oversaw the start of industrialization.

8 Marechal Deodoro da Fonseca
The soldier who overthrew Pedro II declared Brazil a republic in 1889 and became its first president.

9 Getúlio Vargas
President from 1930 to 1945 and again from 1951 to his suicide in 1954. He copied the fascist politics of Europe.

10 Juscelino Kubitschek
Promising 50 years of progress in 5, this president oversaw economic growth but finally bankrupted Brazil.

🔟 Museums and Art Galleries

Oscar Niemeyer's iconic Museu de Arte Contemporanea de Niterói

1 Museu de Arte Contemporanea de Niterói (MAC)

MAP C5 ■ Mirante da Boa Viagem s/n, Boa Viagem, Niterói ■ (21) 2620 2400 ■ Open 10am–6pm Tue–Sun ■ Adm (free on Wed) ■ www.macniteroi.com.br

Contemporary Brazilian art is on display in this museum, which is housed in an iconic building designed by Oscar Niemeyer. The concrete spheroid sits at the end of a rocky promontory that juts into Guanabara Bay, and the interior is accessed via a long red ramp.

2 Museu Histórico Nacional

Housed in a colonial building that served as an arsenal till the 1920s, this fascinating museum charts Brazilian history *(see pp26–7).*

Naïve art on display at the Museu Internacional de Arte Naïf

3 Museu da República

MAP H3 ■ Palácio do Catete, Rua do Catete 153 ■ (21) 2127 0324 ■ Open 10am–5pm Tue–Fri, 11am–6pm Sat, Sun & hols ■ Adm (free on Wed & Sun)

This Baroque palace, now a museum, was the site of the suicide of Brazil's most influential statesman. President Vargas *(see p37)* killed himself in his bedroom here in 1954. Exhibits include his nightshirt, with the bullet hole in the breast.

4 Museu Nacional de Belas Artes

This museum holds the largest collection of Brazilian art in the country, dating from colonial times through to the 20th century. International pieces are also on display here *(see pp20–21).*

5 Museu Internacional de Arte Naïf (MIAN)

MAP G3 ■ Rua Cosme Velho 561, Cosme Velho ■ (21) 2205 8612 ■ Open 10am–6pm Tue–Fri, 10am–5pm Sat & Sun ■ Adm ■ www.museunaif.com

This delightful museum features one the world's largest collections of naïve art. Some of the Brazilian pieces are by *favela* and rural artists and offer powerful insights into their daily lives. There is also an interesting shop in the museum.

6 Estádio do Maracanã

MAP E2 ■ Av Presidente Castelo Branco s/n ■ 0800 062 7222 ■ Open 9am–5pm daily

The pavement outside the world's largest soccer stadium is covered in footprints made by star players, including Pelé. A gallery dedicated to soccer greats is inside the stadium.

7 Museu de Arte Moderna (MAM)

MAP X4 ■ Av Infante Dom Henrique 85, Parque do Flamengo ■ (21) 2240 4944 ■ Open noon–6pm Tue–Fri, 11am–6pm Sat, Sun & hols ■ Adm (free on Wed after 3pm) ■ www.mamrio.org.br

Housed in a modernist building on V-shaped stilts, this museum

features works by local artists such as Tarsila do Amaral and Cândido Portinari (see pp20–21), as well as international artists.

8 Sambódromo and Museu do Carnaval

MAP T4 ■ Rua Marquês de Sapucaí, Praça Onze, Centro ■ Open 11am–5pm Tue–Sun

This stadium, designed by Oscar Niemeyer and built on the street thought to be the birthplace of *samba*, hosts Carnaval parades. Carnaval relics are displayed in the museum.

9 Museu Nacional

MAP E1 ■ Quinta da Boa Vista s/n, São Cristóvão ■ (21) 3938 6900 ■ Open 10am–6pm Tue–Sun, noon–6pm Mon ■ Adm ■ www.museunacional.ufrj.br

This crumbling former palace, set in expansive gardens, preserves a diverse collection of items, including the largest meteorite to fall in Brazil, dinosaur bones, and mummies.

10 Ilha Fiscal

MAP J1 ■ Rua Dom Manuel 15, Praça XV, Centro ■ (21) 2233 9165 ■ Tours: 12:30pm, 2pm, and 3:30pm Sat, Sun & hols ■ Adm

This Neo-Gothic folly was once a 19th-century royal pleasure palace that hosted masked balls that later evolved into Carnaval. It now houses a museum of Brazilian culture.

The bold concrete exterior of the Museu de Arte Moderna

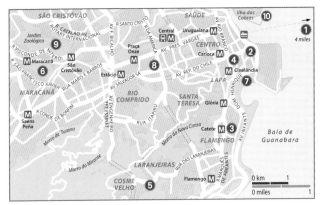

Beaches

1 Ipanema and Leblon
These two contiguous neighborhoods have the cleanest, safest, and most beautiful beaches in the city, and are the favorite playgrounds of Rio de Janeiro's upper-middle class (see pp32–3).

2 Copacabana
From the 1930s to the 1970s, this fine, broad beach was the trendy place to lay a towel in the city. Since the 1980s, it has grown a little tawdry, especially at night. Sunbathing is best in front of the Copacabana Palace hotel (see pp30–31).

3 Charitas
MAP C5

Cariocas are fond of saying that the best thing about Niterói – the city across Guanabara Bay – is its views of Rio. None are better than those from Charitas in the afternoon, when Corcovado and the Sugar Loaf are silhouetted against the setting sun.

4 Botafogo
MAP S1

The Sugar Loaf (see pp16–17) sits at the southern end of this perfectly rounded cove, which lies between Copacabana and Centro, at the mouth of the bay. It was a popular swimming spot until the 1960s, when pollution made bathing inadvisable.

São Conrado and Pedra da Gávea

5 São Conrado
MAP B6

This beach, which is a landing point for hang-gliders, is popular with local television celebrities, many of whom have expensive apartments in the fortified tower blocks that stand between the sea and the city's largest *favela*, Rocinha (see p78).

6 Barra da Tijuca
MAP B6

Rio's largest beach is 11 miles (18 km) long and has both crowded and isolated stretches. It is a favorite with surfers, windsurfers, and fishing enthusiasts. The suburb, known for its many wealthy and famous residents, is characterized by long avenues, apartment blocks, and shopping malls (see p97).

7 Arpoador
MAP P6

This beach around the rocky headland at the southern end of Copacabana features cafés, coconut

Aerial view of Botafogo beach

stalls, and juice bars where *Cariocas* hang out. Strong waves make it popular with surfers but the rocks are unsafe after dark.

Recreio dos Bandeirantes

MAP A6

Despite being very built up, Recreio dos Bandeirantes is a peaceful suburb. The long, straight beach here is pounded by powerful waves, making it a good surf spot.

9 Grumari

MAP A6

Surfers head to this beach at Rio's southern end beyond Barra da Tijuca. The clean waters here are also the coolest in the city. There is a powerful undertow, however, which makes it unsuitable for swimming.

10 Flamengo

MAP Y6

This stretch of pearl-white sand is the prettiest of all the Guanabara Bay beaches and affords wonderful views of the bay and the Sugar Loaf. The water is now far too dirty for swimming and the beach itself is unsafe after dark. The bay is best enjoyed by boat tour; views of Rio from the water are magnificent.

Cycling along Flamengo beach

TOP 10 BRAZILIAN JUICES

Refreshing Camu-Camu juice

1 Açaí
This purple Amazonian palm berry drink has been popular with locals for thousands of years and is becoming trendy around the world. The "superfruit" is packed with vitamins.

2 Cupuaçu
This pod-like fruit is related to cocoa and has a sweet and pungent juice. The taste is unusual but can be strangely addictive.

3 Camu-Camu
This Amazonian fruit grows by seasonally flooded rivers and has a very high vitamin C content.

4 Taperebá
A refreshing Amazonian fruit juice high in vitamin C. It is also supposed to have antibiotic properties.

5 Acerola
Also known as West Indian cherry juice, this is a refreshing and thirst-quenching choice.

6 Graviola
A sweet white juice made from a relative of the custard apple and *caju*.

7 Caju
The juice of the Amazonian cashew-nut fruit, which is also famous the world over for its nuts.

8 Jabuticaba
A tart, berry-like fruit produces a juice popular in the state of Minas Gerais. The fruit grows directly on tree trunks.

9 Umbu
A sweet fruit juice that comes from a pulpy berry. It is particularly popular in the state of Bahia.

10 Seriguela
This refreshing juice comes from Brazil's woodland savannah, the *cerrado*.

TOP 10 Sports and Outdoor Activities

Kite surfers on Praia do Pepê

1 Running

Jogging in the early morning or late afternoon is a favorite *Carioca* pastime. The best places for running are Copacabana, Ipanema, and Leblon.

2 Beach Volleyball

MAP L6 ■ CBV: Rua Carlos Góis, Leblon ■ (21) 98117 3998 ■ Adm for classes ■ www.beachvolleyballrio.com

Ipanema and Copacabana beaches are popular spots to play this game. CBV offers beach volleyball classes.

Beach volleyball on Leblon beach

3 Surfing

ricosurf.globo.com ■ Adm

The best beaches to surf in Rio city are in Ipanema and Leblon – especially at Arpoador beach. Boards can be rented through a school, such as Rico Surf in Barra da Tijuca.

4 Kite Surfing

MAP C2 ■ Forte KiteSurf: Praia do Foguete ■ www. fortekitesurf.com.br ■ Adm

The waves and strong winds to the east of Rio city, beyond Niterói, make this one of the top places for kite surfing. Surfers are attached to kites and dragged through the waves. The best place to learn the sport is in Cabo Frio town, which is 93 miles (148 km) east of Rio.

5 Windsurfing

MAP C2 ■ www.mgwbrasil. com.br

Windsurfing is excellent to the east of Rio, where lagoons and high winds make conditions ideal. MGW Tours offers windsurfing in Niterói.

6 Hang-Gliding and Paragliding

Adm ■ www.justflyinrio.blogspot.com

There are few locations more spectacular for these sports than Rio. Flights launch from the Pedra Bonita *(see p14)* and land at São Conrado beach. Numerous companies offer flights.

7 Hiking
www.rioxtreme.com

The hilly, forested terrain around Rio offers great walking opportunities. One of the best hikes is to the summit of the Pedra da Gávea (see p14), the world's tallest coastal monolith.

8 Rock Climbing
www.climbinrio.com

Rio has many great rock climbs and the views can be fabulous. Top of the list are the Sugar Loaf and Morro da Urca (see pp16–17). Other beautiful but lesser-known locations include Parque Nacional do Itatiaia (see p47) and the Serra dos Órgãos (see p47).

Gávea Golf and Country Club

9 Golf
MAP D6 ▪ Gávea Golf and Country Club: Estrada da Gávea 800, São Conrado ▪ (21) 3323 6050 ▪ Adm

The best golf course in Rio is in Gávea. The 18-hole club is private, but games can be booked through concierges at the better Rio hotels.

10 Diving
MAP C2

Intensive factory fishing in the 1980s has damaged some of the marine life in the waters around Rio. There are still some reasonable dive sites at Arraial do Cabo, near Cabo Frio (see p47), where there is a wealth of soft corals, sponges, and marine life.

TOP 10 OLYMPIC VENUES

Maracanã stadium

1 Rio Olympic Park
The main events site will be converted into an athletics training center, with a lakeside park and boating facilities.

2 Deodoro Olympic Park
The second largest venue; after 2016 it will be rebuilt as X-Park, including whitewater and BMX courses.

3 Maracanã
The world-famous football stadium will host both the opening and closing ceremonies, and football finals.

4 Olympic Golf Course
Golf will be an Olympic event for the first time in 112 years; Barra Golf Club will be the setting.

5 Rio Olympic Arena
The gymnastics base in Barra will be used for major concerts and events.

6 Maria Lenk Aquatic Center
The swimming and diving center in Barra will be kept as a swimming pool and for aquatic events.

7 Sambódromo
Rio's Carnaval parade ground will host archery and the start and finish of the marathon events.

8 Lagoa Rodrigo de Freitas
Rowing and other aquatic events are scheduled to take place on this scenic lagoon.

9 Marina da Glória
Rio's marina will host the sailing events; its environs are getting a makeover, with a park and other public facilities being built.

10 Copacabana
Beach volleyball and aquatic events will take place on Rio's most famous beach, which is being spruced up for the 2016 competition.

Soccer

Estádio do Maracanã hosts matches between Rio's major football clubs

1 Estádio do Maracanã
Once the world's largest soccer stadium, the Maracanã is where Pelé scored his 1,000th goal in 1969. The atmosphere at the stadium during a game is electric (see p39).

2 Flamengo
One of Rio's four big clubs. Its moment of glory was winning the first Brazilian World Championship in 1981. Famous past players include Gérson, Sócrates, and Zico.

Flamengo playing Botafogo

3 Botafogo
This club's ex-players make up a roster of some of the greatest names in Brazilian soccer. Its golden era was in the 1950s and 60s when it provided most of the players for Brazil's victorious World Cup team.

4 Fluminense
Soccer was introduced to Rio de Janeiro by Englishman Oscar Cox, who went on to found Fluminense on July 21, 1902. The club remains one of Rio's most traditional, and many of its supporters are wealthy *Cariocas*. It has an intense rivalry with Flamengo.

5 Vasco da Gama
Named for the Portuguese explorer Vasco da Gama, this club is traditionally supported by Portuguese *Cariocas*.

6 The Rio-vs-São Paulo Tournament
The *Torneio Rio–São Paulo* was a tournament played between teams from the rival states Rio de Janeiro and São Paulo, and was one of the most bitterly contested tournaments. Although it's no longer held, the rivalries still stand.

7 The Rio de Janeiro State Championship

The *Campeonato Carioca*, a competition for the state's soccer clubs, was established in 1906. Fluminense and Flamengo, with more than 30 titles each, have more victories than any other club.

8 The "Maracanazo Tragedy"

"O Maracanaço" refers to the Brazilian soccer "tragedy" during the 1950 World Cup, when Brazil lost to Uruguay. The word has passed into common parlance in Brazil and is used to refer to other soccer defeats and even political debacles.

Late-afternoon beach soccer

9 Beach Soccer
www.fifa.com

Many of Rio's greatest stars learned to play soccer on makeshift pitches on the city's beaches. The players preserved such a love of beach soccer that it is now a FIFA-recognized sport in its own right.

10 Footvolley

This sport began on the beaches of Rio. Its rules are similar to volleyball, but only the feet and head can be used. Brazil remains the leading footvolley team, but is hotly pursued by some Asian nations.

TOP 10 FAMOUS CARIOCA SOCCER STARS

Brazilian superstar Ronaldo

1 Leônidas da Silva (1913–2004)
Before Leônidas da Silva, Brazilian soccer was a white, middle-class game.

2 Nilton Santos (1925–2013)
A key defender in three World Cups and scorer of one of the most spectacular goals of all time in a match against Austria in 1958.

3 Carlos Alberto (b. 1944)
Captain of Brazil's World Cup-winning team in 1970 and a great defender.

4 Garrincha (1933–83)
Pele's contemporary and officially the best Brazilian player other than Pele himself, according to FIFA.

5 Didi (1929–2001)
A legendary midfielder named player of the tournament at the 1958 World Cup in Sweden.

6 Gérson (b. 1941)
One of the best passers in the history of football, who masterminded the 1970 World Cup victory.

7 Zico (b. 1953)
One of the greatest midfielders in the history of the beautiful game.

8 Jairzinho (b. 1944)
A lightning-fast winger who devastated opponents in the 1970 World Cup.

9 Romário (b. 1966)
The only player other than Pelé to score 1,000 goals in professional soccer.

10 Ronaldo (b. 1976)
Nicknamed "The Phenomenon" in Brazil, he won the FIFA Player of the Year award in 1996, 1997, and 2002.

🔟 Off the Beaten Path

Museu Casa do Pontal

1 Museu Casa do Pontal

This museum has a charming collection of ceramic and wooden folk art from all over Brazil. Tiny figurines portray traditional daily life in tableaux that will enchant visitors (see p49).

2 Parque Ecológico Chico Mendes

MAP B6 ■ 679 Av Jarbas do Carvalho, Recreio dos Bandeirantes ■ (21) 2437 6400 ■ Open 8am–6pm Tue–Sun (to 5pm in winter)

This nature reserve offers a taste of tropical wilderness on the doorstep of the city: sandy trails lead through mangroves, marshland and cacti groves; home to endangered caiman, turtles, birds, and butterflies.

3 Ilha Grande

MAP A2

This offshore tropical paradise is two hours west of Rio along the Costa Verde. Empty beaches fringe its shores and jungle trails lead to crystalline waterfalls and lagoons. Boats visit on day cruises, or hop on a ferry from Angra dos Reis port.

4 Sítio Roberto Burle Marx

MAP A6 ■ Estrada Roberto Burle Marx 2019, Barra de Guaratiba ■ (21) 2410 1412 ■ Open 9:30–11:30am & 1:30–3:30pm Tue–Sat (guided tour only, advanced notice required)

The former home of Rio's most celebrated landscape designer; Burle Marx's sculptures dotted around the lush tropical gardens, and the lovingly preserved house contains his personal art collection.

5 Pico da Tijuca

MAP D4 ■ Praça Afonso Viseu, Tijuca ■ (21) 2491 1700 ■ www. amigosdoparque.org.br ■ Open 8am–5pm daily

Hike through the Tijuca National Park to the 1021-m (3,349-ft) summit of Rio's tallest mountain. The final ascent is steep; but your efforts will be rewarded with staggering views. The hike generally starts from 2pm.

Fortaleza de Santa Cruz, Niterói

6 Niterói

This city across the bay may lack its neighbor's natural wonders, but it does have great views of Rio's coastline. The 16th-century Fortaleza de Santa Cruz (Sant Cruz Fort) offers the best vantage point.

7 Valença, Vale do Café

MAP B2 ■ Valença ■ www.preservale.com.br

One of the loveliest old towns in the Vale do Café, deep in Rio state. This used to be at the heart of the

Brazilian coffee empire; its colonial *fazendas* now welcome visitors with tours of the plantations and luxurious accommodation.

⑧ Museu do Bonde, Santa Teresa

MAP V6 ▪ Rua Carlos Brant 14 ▪ (21) 2220 1003 ▪ Open 9am–4pm daily

This tiny museum is dedicated to the rickety old trams that are a symbol of Santa Teresa. On show are early-20th-century trams, together with old photographs and memorabilia, which will appeal to both train-spotters and inquisitive visitors alike.

⑨ Feira de São Cristovão

MAP E1/F1 ▪ Campo de São Cristovão, Centro ▪ (21) 2580 5335 ▪ Open 10am–6pm Tue–Thu, 10am Fri–9pm Sun (24hrs) ▪ www.feiradesaocristovao.org.br

This vast, rambling market in a working-class, downtown neighborhood specializes in all things from northeastern Brazil. Hundreds of stalls are packed with handicrafts, food, and music, and live bands play non-stop all weekend.

⑩ Praia Vermelha

MAP J4 ▪ Praia Vermelha, Urca

This sheltered little beach at the foot of Pão de Açúcar is a family favorite for its calm waters and soft red sand. Nearby are local *por kilo* buffet restaurants, and the start of the Pista Claudio Coutinho walkway *(see p73)*.

Praia Vermelha beach

TOP 10 RIO STATE ATTRACTIONS

Ilha Grande's capital, Abraão

1 Mata Atlântica
MAP B2
Brazil's Atlantic coastal rain forest is home to abundant wildlife.

2 Búzios
MAP B2 ▪ www.buziosonline.com.br
This upscale resort town has beaches backed by restaurants and boutiques.

3 Serra dos Órgãos
MAP B2 ▪ www.riohiking.com
Mountain range northeast of Rio, offering great climbing and trekking.

4 Petrópolis
MAP B2
Home to the Museu Imperial, the former home of the royal family.

5 Teresópolis
MAP B2
This mountain town comes alive on weekends with a bustling artisan fair.

6 Parque Nacional do Itatiaia
MAP A2
Brazil's oldest national park offers superb bird-watching and hiking trails.

7 Região dos Lagos
MAP C2 ▪ www.regiaodos
lagos.com.br
Picturesque coastal region fringed with white, sandy beaches and salt lakes.

8 Cabo Frio
MAP C2
Cariocas come to this popular weekend escape for the beaches, surfing, snorkeling, and scuba diving.

9 Paraty
MAP A3
This beautiful colonial gold-rush town is a UNESCO World Heritage Site.

10 Ilha Grande
MAP A2
Breathtaking beaches and trekking bring people to this road-less island.

🔟 Activities for Children

Baixo Bebê children's play area on Leblon beach

1 Jardim Zoológico
MAP E1 ■ Quinta da Boa Vista, São Cristóvão ■ (21) 3878 4200 ■ Open 9am–4:30pm Tue–Sun (also Mon in summer) ■ Adm ■ www.rio.rj.gov.br/web/riozoo

As well as housing over 2,000 animals, including large carnivores in big enclosures, this smart, modern zoo runs an important captive-breeding program for marmosets and tamarins – the world's smallest monkeys. A little train takes children through the zoo.

2 Parque Nacional da Tijuca

This vast forest park wrapping around Rio contains the city's highest peaks as well as dozens of trails and lookout points, making it an ideal location for a day's hiking and wildlife spotting. It is home to a rich array of wildlife, including monkeys, birds, and butterflies. There are plenty of spots around the park where families can enjoy a picnic in the shade (see pp14–15).

3 Sugar Loaf Mountain

The views from the Sugar Loaf and Morro da Urca may be spectacular, but children will particularly relish the dramatic cable-car rides to the hilltops. The trails on the hills are also worth exploring. Look out for the indigenous tufted-eared marmosets. The Sugar Loaf has a café-bar and Morro da Urca has cafés and restaurants, as well as a theater that hosts popular shows and concerts for all ages (see pp16–17).

4 Baixo Bebê
MAP L6 ■ Leblon beach

This little playground, tucked under the looming Os Dios Irmãos hill at the far end of Leblon beach, has climbing frames and sandpits (see pp32–3). Kids can cool off with coconut milk available at juice stalls nearby. There are child-friendly cafés and restaurants too, in one of Leblon's safest areas.

5 Parque das Ruínas
MAP V5 ■ Rua Murtinho Nobre 169, Santa Teresa ■ (21) 2252 1039 ■ Open 8am–8pm Tue–Sun

Containing ruins of a colonial mansion, this park offers excellent views of the city. There is a gazebo and a small playground for kids to enjoy. It also holds special programs for children over the weekends, with traditional *Carioca* music performances, plays, and exhibitions.

Nijinsky by Mazeredo, Parque da Catacumba

6 Planetário

This state-of-the-art planetarium is one of the best of its kind in South America. As well as astronomical shows (narrated in Portuguese), it has an interesting museum that features touch displays. Kids of all ages are permitted to use the powerful telescopes to view planets and galaxies three times a week *(see p78)*.

7 Rio Water Planet

MAP A6 ■ Estrada dos Bandeirantes, Vargem Grande ■ (21) 2428 9000 ■ Open 10am–5pm Sat–Sun; closed in winter ■ Adm ■ www. riowaterplanet.com.br

The largest collection of water slides, pools, and rides in Rio state are found in Rio Water Planet in the suburb of Vargem Grande, some 12 miles (20 km) from the city center. The best way to visit is by car or taxi as public transport is limited.

8 Parque da Catacumba

This lushly forested, hilly park overlooking Lagoa has a zip-wire adventure trail from raised platforms suspended in the trees. There are different levels suitable for adults and children – all are great fun. Entrance to the park is free, but there is a small charge for the zip-wire trail *(see p77)*.

9 Jardim Botânico

Tucked away behind Lagoa Rodrigo de Freitas, this tropical garden, with its ponds, little streams, and waterfalls, is a lovely place to while away a sunny afternoon. Children will be delighted to spot monkeys and *agoutis* – rabbit-sized rodents that look like tiny deer. Café Botânico sells ice cream *(see pp24–5)*.

Sagui monkey, Jardim Botânico

10 Museu Casa do Pontal

MAP A6 ■ Estrada do Pontal 3295, Recreio dos Bandeirantes ■ (21) 2490 2429 ■ Open 9:30am–5pm Tue–Fri, 10:30am–6pm Sat, Sun & hols; closed during Carnaval Tuesday ■ www.museucasadopontal.com.br

This delightful folk-art museum contains thousands of ceramic and wooden figurines collected from around Brazil. Intricate tableaux portray daily life, from classrooms to carnaval parades.

Figurines in Museu Casa do Pontal

🔟 Restaurants

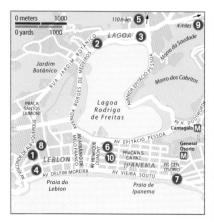

Freitas. The classic French fare makes use of tropical ingredients.

4 Antiquarius
MAP K6 ■ Rua Aristides Espínola 19, Leblon ■ (21) 2294 1049 ■ $$$

One of the city's longest established Portuguese restaurants, Antiquarius oozes old-fashioned style. Celebrities flock here for the famous *bacalhau* (salt-cod) and excellent seafood. The ambience is warm and friendly, though the prices make this a treat for a special occasion.

1 Zuka
MAP K5 ■ Rua Dias Ferreira 233, Leblon ■ (21) 3205 7154 ■ www.zuka.com.br ■ $$$

Decked out in dark wood and fronted by an open grill, this dining room was set up by a former chef of New York's acclaimed restaurant Nobu. It is now run by one of Rio's most celebrated chefs, Ludmilla Soeiro. Zuka's fusion menu comprises grills, seafood, and excellent salads.

2 Roberta Sudbrack
MAP M2 ■ Rua Lineu de Paula Machado 916, Jardim Botânico ■ (21) 3874 0139 ■ www.robertasudbrack.com.br ■ $$$

This eponymous restaurant established Roberta Sudbrack as arguably the best chef in South America. The menu features startlingly original dishes that blend *haute cuisine* with molecular gastronomy in creative ways.

3 Olympe
MAP N2 ■ Rua Custódio Serrão 62, Lagoa ■ (21) 2539 4542 ■ www.olympe. com.br ■ $$$

Claude Troisgros – a pioneer of *nouvelle cuisine* in France – founded this intimate dining room on a quiet street near Lagoa Rodrigo de

5 Satyricon
MAP C2 ■ Av Jose Bento Ribeiro Dantas, Orla Bardot, Búzios ■ (022) 2623 1595 ■ $$$

Satyricon's smart dining room is dominated by a vast counter covered with myriad varieties of tropical fish, crustaceans, and shellfish on ice.

Fresh fish displayed at Satyricon

6 Gero
MAP M5 ■ Rua Aníbal de Mendonça 157, Ipanema ■ (21) 2239 8158 ■ $$$

Set up by celebrated restaurateur Rogério Fasano, this chic, minimalist eatery serves innovative, highly fêted

Tables laid out at sophisticated Fasano

Italian food and has a long bar that dominates the dining room. Its sophisticated clientele come here not only for the dining experience, but also to be seen.

7 Fasano
Rogério Fasano's sophisticated establishment is one of Rio de Janeiro's finest restaurants and is located in one of its most exclusive hotels. Fasano specializes in delicious, fresh seafood and offers exceptionally beautiful views over the Atlantic Ocean *(see p112)*.

8 Manekineko
MAP K5 ▪ Rua Dias Ferreira 410, Leblon ▪ (21) 2540 7461 ▪ $$$
Brazil has more ethnic Japanese than any country in the world outside Japan, and Rio de Janeiro is replete with fine Japanese restaurants. Part of a chain, this restaurant contrasts with the more traditional Sushi Leblon *(see p95)* a few doors away. Brazilian-Japanese fusion cooking is served here to a lively crowd. The menu changes every few months.

9 Espírito Santa
Santa Teresa is full of funky little restaurants and bars, and this is one of the best. Amazonian and Bahian cooking – including exquisite river fish like *pacu* – is served in an informal restaurant-bar and on a small, candle-lit roof terrace, which boasts wonderful views of the city at night. The bartender serves some of Rio's best *caipirinhas* and the club downstairs opens for dancing on Friday nights *(see p86)*.

10 Esplanada Grill
MAP M5 ▪ Rua Barão da Torre 600, Ipanema ▪ (21) 2512 2970 ▪ $$$
Brazil is famous for its grilled meat restaurants, or *churrascarias*, and none is better than the Esplanada Grill. It is a popular place for business men and women who appreciate the high-quality ingredients, large portions, and respectable wine list.

Informal dining at Espírito Santa

For a key to restaurant price ranges see p69

🔟 Bars and Nightclubs

cozy and inviting. The place also offers breathtaking views of Leblon beach. Book in advance.

4 Rio Scenarium

Lapa's plushest *samba* venue hosts live acts downstairs that play standards like *Aquarela do Brasil*, while the club upstairs plays more contemporary Brazilian dance music. There is plenty of quieter sitting space in the gallery areas *(see p86)*. Call ahead for a reservation.

5 Carioca da Gema

Arguably Rio's best live *samba* club, Carioca da Gema is housed in an intimate, converted two-storey town house in Lapa, a short stroll from Rio Scenarium. Some of the best old

1 Academia da Cachaça
MAP L5 ■ Rua Conde de Bernadotte 26G, Leblon
■ (21) 2529 2680

This informal streetside bar has one of the best selections of Brazil's national drink in the city. *Cachaça* is distilled from sugar-cane and is the basis of *caipirinha* cocktails. The bar is liveliest on Friday evenings.

2 Empório
MAP N5 ■ Rua Maria Quitéria 37, Ipanema ■ (21) 3813 2526

Popular among locals and visitors alike, this convivial bar features live music on weekends. The atmosphere is relaxed and the dance floor often shifts to the streets where people gather on sidewalks. The place doesn't get lively until midnight.

3 Restaurante Vizta
MAP L6 ■ Av Delfim Moreira 630, Leblon ■ (21) 2529 5700

Housed inside the Marina Palace hotel, Vizta hosts jazz nights over the weekends (Fri–Sun), each night with a different guest. The atmosphere is

Live *samba* at Rio Scenarium

Crowds dance to the live music at Carioca da Gema

samba and *choro* acts in the city play here. It is a very popular venue and gets crowded on weekends, so go early to ensure you get a table or bar space *(see p86)*.

 Venga!
MAP K5 ▪ Rua Dias Ferreira 113-B ▪ (21) 2512 9826

One of Rio's first Spanish tapas bars, this cozy, busy little place serves small, tasty delicacies, including fresh seafood and vegetarian options; with sangria by the jug or glass, and chilled wine and beer.

⑦ Nuth
MAP B6 ▪ Av Armando Lombardi 999, Barra da Tijuca ▪ (021) 3575 6850 ▪ www.nuth.com.br

This mock-Miami, split-level dance club lies in Barra da Tijuca, half an hour from Ipanema. Enjoy cocktails in the garden or dance to Eurotrash sounds on the packed dance floor. Visit on weekends after 11pm.

⑧ Usina 47t
MAP K6 ▪ Rua Rita Ludolf 47, Leblon ▪ (21) 2249 9309

Hip interiors decorated with exposed-brick walls and wood furnishings welcome guests to this renovated bar that was earlier a nightclub. It offers an extensive list of more than 40 drinks created in-house.

⑨ 00
Stylish and eclectic, 00 (pronounced "zero zero") offers a mixed program of live music and DJs. The little cocktail bar spills into a garden, so it is always possible to find a quiet spot away from the music, if you want a little break.

Diners at Bar Luíz

⑩ Bar Luíz
This long bar-restaurant, with its busy black-tie waiters, has been an after-work institution in Rio for more than 100 years. Famous *Cariocas*, including Heitor Villa-Lobos *(see p72)*, used to come here for a *chopp* (draught beer), *petiscos* (tapas), and conversation, as his modern-day counterparts still do, especially on Friday evenings *(see p68)*.

Shopping

Feira Hippie Market

to The Body Shop, found all over the city. It has a range of superior natural products including tasteful perfumes and aftershaves, many of which are made from scents derived from Brazilian plants.

4 Bikinis from Lenny
MAP N5 ■ Rua Visconde de Pirajá 351 Loja 114/115, Ipanema ■ (21) 2523 3796 ■ www.lenny.com.br
The only place in Rio that has a dress code is the beach. Unless you want to be recognized as a tourist, it is best to wear what the locals wear. Brazilian swimwear is widely regarded as the most fashionable

Blue Man bikini shop

1 Arts and Crafts from the Feira Hippie Market
There is overpriced bric-a-brac in this well-known market in central Ipanema, but also the occasional gem. Look for models of Rocinha houses made of wood or papier-mâché and illuminated from within, and for rope sculptures made by a *favela* artist (see p94).

2 Northeastern Arts and Crafts from Feira de São Cristóvão
MAP E1 ■ Centro Luiz Gonzaga de Tradições Nordestinos, Campo de São Cristóvão ■ (21) 2580 0501 ■ Open 10am–4pm Tue–Thu and non-stop 10am Fri–10pm Sun ■ www.feiradesao cristovao.org.br
It is worth coming to this vast, bustling market as much for the *forró* music and the spectacle, as it is for the arts and crafts and delicious, fresh northeastern food.

3 Perfume from O Boticário
MAP W3 ■ www. oboticario.com.br
O Boticário is a Brazilian chain of cosmetic and body-care shops, similar

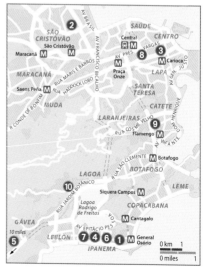

Feather headdress from Casa Turuna

in the world – at least by fashionistas and models – and the best place to find the most trendy cuts and patterns is in the heart of Ipanema, at Lenny. There are many other stores nearby, including Salinas and Blue Man.

5 Coffee from Garcia and Rodrigues

MAP B6 ▪ Barra Shopping, Av das Américas 4666 ▪ (21) 2431 8291 ▪ www.garciaerodrigues.com.br
This swanky bakery and coffee shop serves light meals, salads, and great coffee. The coffee is also available to buy ready-ground to take home.

6 Jewelry from Antônio Bernardo

MAP M5 ▪ Rua Garcia D'Avila, Ipanema ▪ (21) 2512 7204 ▪ www.antoniobernardo.com.br
Brazil's most stylish and exclusive jeweler has branches worldwide, but the best choice is still to be found in Brazil where it all began. This is the award-winning jeweler's flagship shop, where buying a pair of earrings can set you back $2,000.

7 Books from Livraria da Travessa

MAP N5 ▪ Rua Visconde de Pirajá 572, Ipanema (one of seven branches) ▪ (21) 3205 9002 ▪ www.travessa.com.br
The charming Livraria da Travessa offers a wide selection of Brazilian and international books, music DVDs, and great coffee.

8 Carnaval Costumes from Casa Turuna

MAP W2 ▪ Rua Senhor dos Passos 124, Centro ▪ (21) 2509 3908
Those wanting to take a bit of Carnaval color home or to dress themselves up during Carnaval week should head to this store in Centro. It sells everything from feather boas to sequin bikinis at reasonable prices.

9 Crafts from Pé de Boi

MAP W6 ▪ Rua Ipiranga 53, Laranjeiras ▪ (21) 2285 4385 ▪ Open 9am–7pm Mon–Fri, 9am–1pm Sat ▪ www.pedeboi.com.br
This ethically conscious shop sells handicrafts sourced from artisans across Brazil, with a huge range of beautiful handmade products, from painted ceramics to woven baskets and naïve-style artworks.

10 Crafts from Parceria Carioca

MAP E5 ▪ Rua Jardim Botânico 728 ▪ (21) 2259 1437 ▪ www.parceriacarioca.com.br
This great shop sells fun and funky accessories and crafts made by local cooperatives in some of Rio's poorest neighborhoods. The proceeds help to fund artisan workshops.

Parceria Carioca storefront

Rio de Janeiro for Free

View of Sugar Loaf Mountain, Morro da Urca, and Botafogo

1 Museums

Centro Cultural Banco do Brasil: Rua Primeiro de Março 66, Centro ▪ 9am–9pm Wed–Mon ▪ (21) 3808 2020 ▪ culturabancodobrasil.com.br/portal/rio-de-janeiro/

Many of Rio's museums are free on Sunday, and some are always free, including the Centro Cultural Banco do Brasil, Oi Futuro (see p74), and the Paço Imperial (see p29).

2 Sunset over Ipanema

Join the locals on Ipanema beach at the end of every day, when they gather to watch the sun setting over Dois Irmãos, applauding and toasting as darkness falls.

3 Free Guided Walks

www.freewalkertours.com ▪ No booking required ▪ Mon–Sat

Take a free walking tour of the city, led by locals with expert knowledge of *Carioca* culture and history. Tours are in English and Portuguese. Three different tours cover Downtown and Lapa, Copacabana and Ipanema, and a night-time "pub crawl" of Lapa.

4 Capoeira

www.lagoaazulcapoeira.com

Popular all over Brazil, this hypno-tically acrobatic dance is actually a martial art, developed in north-eastern Brazil hundreds of years ago by slaves from Africa. You can enjoy free *capoeira* displays at the Parque Patins in Lagoa on Monday, Wednesday, and Friday evenings.

5 Escadaria Selarón

The colorful steps leading from Lapa to Santa Teresa were the work of eccentric Chilean artist Jorge Selarón (1947–2013). He spent the last 20 years of his life creating this tribute to the area (see p84).

Colorful Escadaria Selarón

6 Parks and Gardens

Rio is a gloriously green city. As well as the jungle backdrop that is the free Parque Nacional da Tijuca (see p14–15), there are many free parks and gardens, including Parque do Flamengo (see p74), Parque Lage (see p78), and Parque Ecológico Chico Mendes (see p98).

7 Beach Activities

Rio's magnificent beaches are huge free playgrounds. You can flex your muscles at the workout stations, watch – or dare to join – a football or volleyball game, and see displays of sand sculptures.

Music

Pedra do Sal: Largo João da Baiana, Praça Mauá, Saúde ■ www.mapadecultura.rj.gov.br/manchete/roda-de-samba-da-pedra-do-sal ■ **Open from 8pm Mon & Fri**

Cariocas live and breathe to a musical rhythm; singing and dancing can break out at any bar day and night. There are free concerts all weekend at the Feira de São Cristovão *(see p54)* and free samba on Monday nights in Pedra do Sal, a tiny square in Saúde.

City Views

Soak up stunning panoramas of Rio from its many hilltop *mirantes* (lookouts). Check out Tijuca National Park *(see pp14–15)*; Parque da Catacumba *(see p77)*, overlooking Lagoa; and Morro da Urca *(see p16–17)*, reached via a (steep) trail off the Pista Claudio Coutinho.

Churches

Most of Rio's churches are free to enter. There are some spectacular architectural wonders, including Mosteiro de São Bento *(see pp18–19)*, Igreja Santo Antônio *(see p66)*, and Catedral Metropolitana *(see p66)*.

Catedral Metropolitana

Carnaval Parades and Balls

A colorful float at the Sambódromo during Carnaval

1 Sunday and Monday at the Sambódromo

MAP T4 ▪ **Centro** ▪ **Adm**

On the first Sunday and Monday of Carnaval, the top *samba* schools march through the Sambódromo *(see p39)* in *blocos* (parades) to compete for the title of champion.

2 Banda de Ipanema

This is one of Carnaval's largest and most colorful street parades. Outrageously dressed transvestite and transsexual party-goers dance *samba* with tourists, families, and passersby *(see p107)*.

3 Baile do Copa

MAP R3 ▪ **Copacabana** ▪ **Adm**

Another Carnaval tradition is the formal "Russian Imperial" black-tie ball, which is held at the Copacabana Palace hotel *(see p112)* on the first Saturday of Carnaval. Book tickets through the hotel in advance.

4 Blocos in Santa Teresa

MAP U5 ▪ **Santa Teresa** ▪ **Adm**

The highlights of this lively street party are its atmosphere and music. It takes place on a stretch between Largo dos Guimarães and Largo das Neves in Santa Teresa, and is popular with a young crowd.

5 Champions' Parade

MAP T4 ▪ **Centro** ▪ **(21) 4042 0213** ▪ **Adm**

The winners of the spectacular Sambódromo parades dance again on the final Saturday of Carnaval. It is easier to get tickets for this event than the earlier performances.

6 Bloco Cacique de Ramos

MAP W1–W3 ▪ **Centro** ▪ **(21) 3880 9248** ▪ **Adm**

The Bloco Cacique de Ramos parade has marched along Avenida Rio Branco since 1961. A new *samba* song is written and sung every year by one of Rio's famed *sambistas*.

7 Bloco de Segunda

MAP Q1 ▪ **Botafogo**

Held on the first Monday of Carnaval week, this *bloco* features dancers in elaborate costumes, including *Baianas* (Afro-Brazilian women) in enormous flowing dresses who spin as they *samba* along Rua Marques.

8 Viemos do Egypto
MAP X4 ■ Centro

A hit with a younger LGBT crowd dressed as pharaohs and Cleopatras, this is one of the more recent *blocos* on the scene. Viemos do Egypto was originally a nightclub party that migrated to the streets for Carnaval, something that also happens the other way around throughout the year. The *bloco* is found at Cinelândia metro station on Carnaval Tuesday.

9 Baile Vermelho e Preto do Flamengo
MAP Q1 ■ Botafogo ■ (21) 2512 8833 ■ Adm

Vermelho (red) and *preto* (black) are the colors of one of Rio's most popular soccer teams, Flamengo (see p44), and are a compulsory part of the dress code at their annual ball held at the Clube Monte Líbano in Lagoa. Costumes are notoriously skimpy and the *sambas* recount past football glories.

10 Gala Gay
One of Rio's most famous and lavish indoor Carnaval balls takes place at a different location each year on Carnaval Tuesday. The star-studded event is heavily televised globally and tickets are incredibly hard to secure (see p107).

Carnaval float decorations

TOP 10 SAMBA SCHOOLS

Beija Flor de Nilópolis *samba* school

1 Portela
www.sambacity.info/portela.html
This school has won the Sambódromo *samba* contest 21 times under a blue and white flag.

2 Mangueira
www.mangueira.com br
This popular school has won 17 times. Its colors are pink and green.

3 Império Serrano
Parading under a green flag, Serrano has had nine victories.

4 Unidos da Tijuca
www.unidosdatijuca.com.br
Winner of multiple gold standards, Tijuca's colors are yellow and blue.

5 Unidos do Viradouro
The famous Carnaval queen Juliana Paes danced for this school. Orange and white are its colors.

6 Salgueiro
www.salgueiro.com.br
A top school with nine victories, colored red and white.

7 Estácio de Sá
www.gresestaciodesa.com.br
One-time victors in 1992, its colors are red and white.

8 Imperatriz Leopoldinense
www.imperatrizleopoldinense.com.br
A successful school with eight victories, its colors are green, yellow, and white.

9 Beija Flor de Nilópolis
www.beija-flor.com.br
Flying a blue and white flag, this is the most successful school since 2000, with 13 wins.

10 Vila Isabel
www.gresunidosdevilaisabel.com.br
With three victories to date, this club flies the peach and white flag.

🔟 Festivals and Shows

Performer at Carnaval

① New Year's Eve
Dec 31

Rio's biggest celebration is not Carnaval but Reveillon, or New Year's Eve. Millions of people gather on Copacabana beach for the party, with free concerts and spectacular fireworks displays *(see p30)*.

② Carnaval
MAP T4 ▪ Sambódromo, Rua Marquês de Sapucaí, Centro ▪ (21) 3213 5151 ▪ Feb/Mar ▪ Adm

Carnaval takes place at the start of Lent in February or March. The parades take place in Oscar Niemeyer's Sambódromo stadium.

③ The Festa de Nossa Senhora da Penha
MAP D3 ▪ Largo da Penha 19, Penha ▪ (21) 3219 6262 ▪ Oct ▪ www.santuariopenhario.org.br

Catholic pilgrims crawl or walk on their knees up the steps to this church for the city's most traditional festival.

④ Festas Juninas
Jun

These extensive religious festivals are held throughout June in homage to St. Anthony and St. John. Locals dress up in checked shirts, drink spicy wine, feast on traditional food, and dance to lively *forró* music.

⑤ Presente de Yemanjá
Dec 31

This New Year's Eve celebration is dedicated to Yemanjá the Orixá, the Goddess of the Sea. Devotees dressed in white gather on beaches around the city from midnight until dawn to worship her and toss offerings in the Atlantic.

⑥ Festa de São Sebastião
Jan 20

The patron saint of Rio is honored with a series of processions that leave from the church of São Sebastião dos Capuchinhos in Tijuca and make their way to the city center.

New Year's Eve fireworks above the beach at Copacabana

(7) Festa Literária Internacional de Paraty

Jul/Aug ■ www.flip.org.br

This gathering of acclaimed international writers takes place in the pretty little colonial port town of Paraty, which is located three hours south of Rio de Janeiro. There is always plenty of live music and other events on offer here. Past guests have included well-known novelists such as Toni Morrison, Salman Rushdie, and Michael Ondaatje.

Festa Literária Internacional de Paraty

(8) Festival Internacional de Cinema do Rio

Sep–Oct ■ www.festivaldorio.com.br

One of South America's largest and most diverse film festivals, this event showcases independent films from all over the world, with a special focus on Latin America. Full features and shorts are shown in cinemas throughout the city.

(9) Anima Mundi – Festival Internacional de Cinema de Animação

Jul ■ www.animamundi.com.br

One of the world's premier celebrations of animation showcases work from mainstream, independent, and avant-garde film-makers from all over the world. Every year, after the festival takes place in Rio, it moves on south to São Paulo.

(10) Dia do Índio

Apr 19

This celebration commemorates the first Inter-American Indigenous Congress, which took place in Mexico City in 1940. Indigenous people from all over Brazil participate.

TOP 10 LIVE ACTS IN RIO

1 Jorge Ben
The founding father of the funky Rio sound plays live on New Year's Eve.

2 Roberto Carlos
Year-end festivities in Rio would not be complete without a show by Latin America's most successful recording artist.

3 Orquestra Imperial
Made up of popular local musicians, this dance-hall *samba*, or *gafieira*, band is a Carnaval party stalwart.

4 Chico Buarque
The political conscience of his generation, Buarque sometimes performs gigs in Lapa.

5 Cidade Negra
Brazil's top reggae band regularly plays to huge audiences over New Year and during Carnaval.

6 Sandra de Sá
The queen of Rio *samba* soul is famous for her covers of classic Motown tracks and is another festival regular.

7 Martinho da Vila
Writer of many of the official Carnaval parade *sambas* for the Unidos de Vila Isabel *samba* school.

8 Zeca Pagodinho
The king of Rio party music plays an infectious variant of *samba* called *pagode*.

9 Seu Jorge
One of Brazil's biggest music and movie stars who made his name at the Circo Voador *(see p86)* club in Lapa.

10 Marisa Monte
A trained classical musician, Monte has become one of Rio de Janeiro's biggest international stars.

Cidade Negra

Top 10 Rio de Janeiro Area by Area

Cable car carrying visitors to the top of Sugar Loaf Mountain

🔟 Centro

Rio's bustling city center sits on a promontory that juts out into Guanabara Bay. A wave of rash construction in the early 20th century led to many of the area's finest buildings being razed to the ground, and the center lost much of the architectural unity. However, reminders of Rio's grand past can

Tiles, Igreja Santo Antônio

still be found around Centro's broad avenues, where modern buildings are interspersed with delightful palaces and Baroque churches, as well as fascinating museums and art galleries.

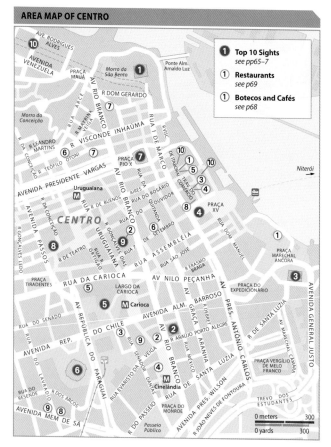

AREA MAP OF CENTRO

1 **Top 10 Sights**
see pp65–7

1 **Restaurants**
see p69

1 **Botecos and Cafés**
see p68

Interior of Igreja de Nossa Senhora do Monte do Carmo, Praça XV

1 Mosteiro de São Bento

Rio's oldest church is also one of Brazil's most beautiful. Its modest facade belies a lavish interior of Baroque carvings, including an opulent Blessed Sacrament Chapel. If you visit on Sundays at 10am, you can hear the Benedictine monks, who live in the adjacent monastery, singing a Latin mass *(see pp18–19)*.

2 Museu Nacional de Belas Artes

Rio's foremost art gallery houses one of Latin America's most impressive collections. Vitor Meirelles' apology for colonialism, *A Primeira Missa no Brasil*, is displayed here. Arguably more interesting Modernist Brazilian work is represented by painters such as Cândido Portinari, Emiliano Di Cavalcanti, and the *antropofagista* Tarsila do Amaral, who defined the modern Brazilian style *(see pp20–21)*.

3 Museu Histórico Nacional

Devoted entirely to the history of Brazil, Museu Histórico Nacional is one of the largest museums in the country. Panels and displays trace the development of Brazil from the Stone Age, when the first inhabitants left paintings in the Serra da Capivara, up until the first days of the republic. A café next to the lobby serves delicious coffee, fresh juices, and snacks. Visit during the week or early in the morning to avoid the crowds *(see pp26–7)*.

4 Praça XV

Dominated by the Paço Imperial, this flagstone square next to the ferry port preserves the memory of Rio under Portuguese rule. Until the Proclamation of the Republic in 1889, this square was the political center of Rio and Minas Gerais, and after the arrival of the royal family, it was the seat of power for Brazil. Praça XV is home to historic buildings, restaurants, shops, and two of central Rio's finest churches – Igreja de Nossa Senhora do Monte do Carmo and Igreja da Ordem Terceira de Nossa Senhora Carmo da Antiga Sé *(see pp28–9)*.

Rock paintings at the Museu Histórico Nacional

Catedral Metropolitana de São Sebastião

BOTECOS

The little restaurants and bars that dot the city from Ipanema to the center are called *botecos* or *botequins*. All are busy with waiters rushing around carrying glasses of frothy ice-cold beer and light snacks. The most famous *botecos* in the center are Bar Luíz *(see p53)* and Garota de Ipanema *(see p92)*, where *bossa nova* was popularized in the early 1960s.

5 Igreja Santo Antônio

MAP W3 ▪ Largo da Carioca s/n ▪ (21) 2262 0129 ▪ Open 8am–6:30pm Mon–Fri, 8–11am, 2:30–6pm Sat, 9:30–11:30am Sun

Rio's second-oldest convent is set in a series of beautiful colonial churches on a hill overlooking Largo da Carioca. The bright interior is decorated with tiles and statues of St. Anthony. Women are often seen praying to the saint, who is said to be a provider of husbands.

6 Catedral Metropolitana de São Sebastião

MAP W4 ▪ Av República do Chile 245 ▪ (21) 2240 2669 ▪ Open 7am–5pm daily (museum 9am–noon Wed, Sat & Sun; also 1–4pm Wed) ▪ www.catedral.com.br

The impressive Modernist Catedral Metropolitana was built by Edgar de Oliveira da Fonseca in 1976–84. The basement houses a Sacred Art Museum preserving age-old artifacts of the Portuguese royal family.

7 Candelária Church

MAP W2 ▪ Praca Pio X ▪ (21) 2233 2324 ▪ Open 7:30am–3:30pm Mon–Fri, 9am–noon Sat, 9am–1pm Sun

This grand Italianate temple has long been the church of choice for high-society Rio. Built between 1775 and 1894, the church was modeled on Lisbon's Basílica da Estrela; the marble for the interior was shipped from Verona. The Candelária gets its name from a chapel built in homage to Our Lady of Candles, which stood on the same site from 1610.

8 Real Gabinete Português de Leitura

MAP W3 ▪ Rua Luís de Camões 30 ▪ (21) 2221 3138 ▪ Open 9am–6pm Mon–Fri ▪ www.realgabinete.com.br

This splendid library is a hidden treasure in the city center. The

Interior of Candelária Church

Manueline style evolved in Portugal in the 15th century and is unique because of its Islamic influences and nautical motifs. The library was built in the 19th century by the Portuguese architect Rafael da Silva e Castro, and is thought to house the biggest collection of Portuguese literary works outside Portugal.

9 Confeitaria Colombo

MAP W2 ■ Rua Gonçalves Dias 32 ■ (21) 2505 1500 ■ Open 9am–7:30pm Mon–Fri, 9am–7pm Sat ■ www.confeitariacolombo.com.br

This excellent bakery-tea house is few blocks from the Real Gabinete. The lower gallery features towering mirrors, while the upper gallery is brightened by a delightful Art Nouveau skylight. The *feijoada (see p110)* colonial lunch on Saturdays is often accompanied by live music. There is another branch of Confeitaria Colombo at Forte de Copacabana *(see p30)*.

Confeitaria Colombo

10 Porto Maravilha

Porto Maravilha, Gamboa ■ www.portomaravilha.com.br

Rio's docks are having a multi-billion Real makeover, transforming the downtown district into a gleaming new hub. One of the city's biggest-ever regeneration projects will see waterfront parks, museums, hotels, restaurants, and shops being erected over the next 15 years.

A DAY IN THE HISTORIC CENTER

▶ MORNING

Begin with a visit to a temporary exhibition in the **Paço Imperial** *(see p29)* or the fine churches that cluster around nearby **Praça XV** *(see pp28–9)*. There is often some interesting bric-a-brac in the little market on the square and the shop inside the **Paço Imperial** is great for browsing. Walk north across the square under the **Arcos de Teles** archway and along the charming **Travessa do Comércio** *(see p29)*. Cross Rua 1 de Março to visit the grand **Candelária Church** then head back to Rua Ouvidor. The streets off Ouvidor throng with activity and give a real feel of Rio's working life. Next, take a left onto Rua Gonçalves Dias and have lunch at the **Confeitaria Colombo** at No. 32.

AFTERNOON

The magnificent **Real Gabinete Português de Leitura** is close by. To reach it, walk back up Rua Gonçalves Dias and turn left onto Rua Ouvidor – it is just after the São Francisco de Paula church on the right. Then head south along Rua Ramalho Ortigão to the Largo da Carioca and the Baroque **Igreja Santo Antônio**, which is on a hill. You will see the cone of **Catedral Metropolitana de São Sebastião** from here. The **Teatro Municipal** is east along Avenida República do Chile. From here, it is a stroll across Avenida Rio Branco to the **Museu Nacional de Belas Artes** *(see pp20–21)* or the **Amarelinho** boteco *(see p68)* for a *chopp* beer.

See map on p64 →

Botecos and Cafés

1 Casa Timão
MAP X2 ■ Rua Visconde de Itaboraí 10 ■ (21) 2224 9616

Decorated with nautical relics and illuminated by a 19th-century French chandelier, this bar attracts a lively after-work crowd.

2 Confeitaria Colombo
This grand Portuguese coffee shop, which doubles up as a *boteco*, serves various snacks as well as sweet cakes *(see p67)*.

3 Botecos on Travessa do Comércio
MAP X2

The *botecos* that line this alley by Praça XV *(see pp28–9)* are a favorite haunt for *Cariocas* in search of cold beer, tasty snacks, and great atmosphere after work.

Botecos on Travessa do Comércio

4 Amarelinho
MAP X4 ■ Praça Floriano 55B ■ (21) 3549 8434

This bright yellow *boteco* has been here since the early 20th century. The best tables have a partial view of Sugar Loaf Mountain.

5 Bar Luíz
MAP W3 ■ Rua da Carioca 39 ■ (21) 2262 6900

Rio's most famous and celebrated *boteco* has been serving delicious German beer and snacks since 1887.

Casa Timão

6 O Paladino
MAP W2 ■ Rua Uruguaiana 226 ■ (21) 2263 2094

One of Centro's most traditional *botecos* often plays live music at night. Try the prawn *pestico*.

7 Botecos on Beco das Sardinhas
MAP W2 ■ Rua Miguel Couto

Wander around this bustling pedestrian street, sampling beers and snacks from its *botecos* as you go.

8 Belmonte Lapa
MAP W4 ■ Av Mem de Sá 82 ■ (21) 2224 2169

This fun and lively bar is popular with Lapa's young arty crowd. Try the ultra-chilled *chopp* draft beer with some tasty *petiscos* (tapas).

9 Bar Brasil
MAP W4 ■ Av Mem de Sá 90 ■ (21) 2509 5943

This German *boteco* offers a range of Bavarian food and beer. The paintings are by Selarón, who decorated the Ladeira de Selarón *(see p84)*.

10 Rio Minho
MAP W2 ■ Rua do Ouvidor 10 ■ (21) 2509 2338

Excellent seafood is on offer in this *boteco*-restaurant, famous for its loyal clientele. Popular at lunchtime.

Restaurants

Albamar
MAP X2 ▪ Praça Marechal Âncora ▪ (21) 2240 8378 ▪ $$$

Once part of a large market that was demolished in 1933, this tower restaurant, which serves delicious seafood, was so popular with Rio's high society that it survived.

② Restaurante Assyrius
MAP X3 ▪ Theatro Municipal, Praça Floriano s/n ▪ (21) 2262 3935 ▪ Closed for dinner ▪ $

This popular lunchtime spot offers excellent coffee, cakes, and snacks.

③ Brasserie Europa
MAP W4 ▪ Rua Senador Dantas 117 ▪ (21) 2220 2656 ▪ $

Executives come here to lunch in air-conditioned comfort on weekdays over ice-cold beers.

Makoto
MAP X2 ▪ Travessa do Comércio 15 ▪ (21) 2224 0338 ▪ Closed for dinner, Sun ▪ $$$

This little Japanese restaurant and cocktail bar also offers the *por kilo* system at weekends, with local dishes including *feijoada*. Live *samba* bands play on Saturday afternoons.

Simple interior of Bistro do Paço

PRICE CATEGORIES
For a three-course meal for one with half a bottle of wine, taxes, and extra charges. Prices quoted in US dollars.

$ under $25 $$ $25–50 $$$ over $50

⑤ Cais do Oriente
MAP X2 ▪ Rua Visconde de Itaboraí 8 ▪ (21) 2233 2531 ▪ $

One of Centro's most lavish restaurants serves Brazilian versions of Asian and Mediterranean dishes. The prices are very reasonable. There is live *samba* and *choro* on weekends.

⑥ 14 Folhas
MAP W3 ▪ Rua Sete de Setembro 48 ▪ (21) 2242 9009 ▪ $

Healthy sandwiches and snacks are the draw at this buffet restaurant.

⑦ Mosteiro
MAP W1 ▪ Rua São Bento 13/15 ▪ (21) 2233 6426 ▪ $$$

Named in honor of the nearby Mosteiro de São Bento *(see pp18–19)*, this traditional restaurant is famous for its *bacalhau* (salted cod).

⑧ Bistro do Paço
MAP X2 ▪ Paço Imperial, Praça XV ▪ (21) 2262 3613 ▪ $

Located in the central atrium of the Paço Imperial *(see p29)*, this bistro has a menu of light lunches.

⑨ Al-Kuwait
MAP X4 ▪ Av Treze de Maio 23 ▪ (21) 2240 1114 ▪ $

The menu at this immensely popular and good-value Arabic and North African restaurant also includes some Brazilian fare.

⑩ Bistrô dos Correios
MAP X2 ▪ Rua Visconde de Itaboraí 20 ▪ (21) 2219 5324 ▪ Open noon–7pm ▪ $

Tucked inside the Centro Cultural Dos Correios and handy for its exhibitions, this smart bistro is good for lunch, a snack, or a delicious afternoon tea.

See map on p64

🔟 The Guanabara Bay Beach Neighborhoods

War Memorial in Glória

The history of fashionable Rio can be traced through a series of beach neighborhoods that line Guanabara Bay. In colonial times, the aristocracy frequented Centro, then Glória, with its yacht-filled harbor, and, in the mid-20th century, Flamengo and Botafogo. When the water became polluted, they headed for Copacabana. Today, Ipanema and Leblon are the places to be, but the bay neighborhoods retain stately buildings, attractive parks, and interesting little museums and galleries.

AREA MAP OF THE GUANABARA BAY BEACH NEIGHBORHOODS

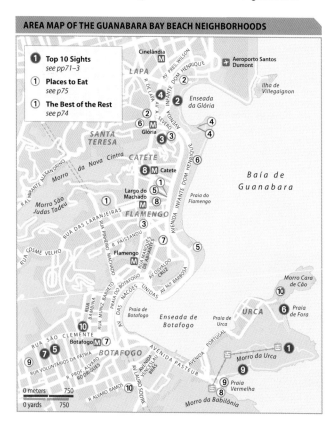

Sugar Loaf Mountain and Morro da Urca, with Botafogo in the foreground

1 Sugar Loaf Mountain

This famous peak sits in Guanabara Bay, staring out toward Niterói and the inky-blue Atlantic. The view from the top is as breathtaking as from Cristo Redentor and looks best in the early morning. The first European reached the summit in 1817. Nowadays, it is far easier to get there – by cable car, helicopter, or hiking trail (see pp16–17).

2 Monumento Nacional aos Mortos da II Guerra Mundial (War Memorial)

MAP X5 ■ Av Infante Dom Henrique 75, Glória ■ (21) 2240 1283 ■ Open 10am–5pm Tue–Sun

This beautifully balanced plinth supports two concrete columns topped by a convex slab, and is one of Rio's most impressive Modernist monuments. It was designed by architects Marcos Konder Neto and Hélio Ribas Marinho in 1952 to commemorate the Brazilian soldiers who were killed in fighting in Italy during World War II.

3 Igreja Nossa Senhora da Glória do Outeiro

MAP X6 ■ Praça Nossa Senhora da Glória 135, Glória ■ (21) 2225 2869 ■ Open 9am–noon and 1–5pm Tue–Fri, 9am–noon Sat & Sun ■ Adm

One of the prettiest 18th-century churches in Rio is perched on a little hill surrounded by woods, and overlooks the bay. The polygonal interior, lined with fine painted blue and white *azulejo* tiles, is impressive. The church was the favorite of the Brazilian royal family. Emperor Dom Pedro II (see p37) was baptized here.

4 Praça Paris

MAP X5 ■ Av Augusto Severo, Glória

Located between Glória, Lapa, and Centro, this leafy square is an ideal place to take a leisurely walk among fountains and statues. It was designed by Alfredo Agache, taking inspiration from the French gardens of the early 20th century. Be careful while using cameras and smartphones as muggings happen in this area.

Igreja Nossa Senhora da Glória do Outeiro interior

Heitor Villa-Lobos

5 Museu Villa-Lobos

MAP Q1 ■ Rua Sorocaba 200, Botafogo ■ (21) 2226 9818 ■ Open 10am–5pm Mon–Fri ■ www.museuvillalobos.org.br

Heitor Villa-Lobos is Latin America's most highly respected classical composer. Between 1917 and his death in 1959, he produced over 1,000 highly original works influenced by both foreign composers and Brazilian musical styles, particularly *choro*. His best-known piece is the *Bachianas Brasileiras*, which pays homage to both Bach and Brazilian folk music. The museum in the musician's former home is devoted to displays of his personal effects. These include many of his musical instruments, manuscripts, and recordings. The museum also hosts performances of his music.

6 Praia de Fora

MAP J4 ■ Urca

This fabulous beach is huddled between the base of the Morro Cara de Cão and the Sugar Loaf. It was here that Estácio de Sá and his men disembarked on March 1, 1565, and founded the city of São Sebastião do Rio de Janeiro. It is regarded as one of the safest beaches in Rio and is frequented by locals having valid admission cards. Since it is a property of the army, you will need permission to get in. Call (21) 2586 2291 to book ahead.

7 Museu do Índio

MAP Q1 ■ Rua das Palmeiras 55, Botafogo ■ (21) 3214 8700 ■ Open 9am–5:30pm Tue–Fri, 1–5pm Sat, Sun & hols ■ www.museudoindio.gov.br

When the Europeans arrived, Brazil was inhabited by over 5 million indigenous people divided into at least 1,000 groups. Much of their culture was wiped out with the onset of slavery. This museum displays many indigenous objects and has rooms devoted to information panels and slide shows. There is also a *Guaraní maloca* (communal thatch house), a gift shop, and a library.

8 Museu de Folclore Edison Carneiro

MAP H3 ■ Rua do Catete 179–181, Catete ■ (21) 2285 0441 ■ Open 11am–6pm Tue–Fri, 3–6pm Sat & Sun

Established in 1968, the Museum of Folklore displays arts and crafts from all over Brazil. The comprehensive museum features carved

Secluded Praia de Fora, seen from Sugar Loaf Mountain

models and tableaus of rodeos, circuses, and festival scenes, which, when switched on, work like music boxes. Over 14,000 exhibits, including bibliographic documents, audiovisual displays, and hundreds of ceramic objects and photographs, paint a vivid picture of Brazil's cultural life.

Museu de Folclore Edison Carneiro

9 Pista Cláudio Coutinho
MAP J4 ■ Open 6am–6pm daily

This walking track snakes its way around the base of the Sugar Loaf and Morro da Urca, and then up to the top of Morro da Urca. The views are wonderful throughout. The trail cuts through woodland filled with tiny, tufted-eared marmosets and brilliantly colored tanagers, and dips onto the Praia de Fora beach. Walks are coolest in the early morning, and the trail is one of the safest in urban Rio because of the huge army presence in Urca.

10 Casa de Rui Barbosa
MAP Q1 ■ Rua São Clemente 134, Botafogo ■ (21) 3289 4600 ■ Open 9am–5:30pm Tue–Fri, 2–6pm Sat–Sun & hols ■ Adm (free on Sun) ■ www.casaruibarbosa.gov.br

Rui Barbosa was one of the most influential politicians in the early years of the Brazilian republic. His former home, one of many stately 19th-century town houses to have been preserved in Botafogo, is now a museum. There are often free classical music concerts in the main hall and the gardens are an oasis of peace and quiet away from the bustle of busy Botafogo.

A CLIMB UP MORRO DA URCA AND THE SUGAR LOAF

The sides of the twin boulder mountains of **Morro da Urca** and the **Sugar Loaf** (see pp16–17) look impossibly steep. But there is an easy path leading to the summit of Urca and a more challenging trail to the top of the **Sugar Loaf**. The trail at the foot of Urca is known as the **Pista Cláudio Coutinho**. This is guarded by a small gateway that is opened between 7am and 8am every morning. Look for the signpost at the eastern end of Praia Vermelha in Urca. The flat, paved path winds around the base of the **Sugar Loaf**, right next to the indigo water of Guanabara Bay. After about 330 yards (300 m), a signpost leads the way up the steep mountainside to the top of Urca. Before long, it becomes possible to see right across Guanabara Bay to the city center. The summit of Urca takes about an hour to reach from the start.

Bring plenty of water, a camera, sun protection, and a hat. Cool off beneath the trees or in the cafés at the top of **Morro da Urca**. The path up the **Sugar Loaf** is more difficult to access, and some stretches must be climbed. It is possible to climb the mountain with a tour company like Rio Hiking. It usually takes around two hours to reach the summit.

At the top of Morro da Urca

See map on p70 ←

The Best of the Rest

1 Parque Guinle
MAP G3/H3 ■ Rua Gago Coutinho 66, Laranjeiras ■ Open 24hrs daily

This peaceful little park is a popular picnic spot for local families, with a playground and duck pond. Only the ornate gates remain of the original owner's stately residence.

2 Chafariz da Glória
MAP X2 ■ Rua de Glória 156

Built in 1772, this is one of the city's oldest public drinking fountains. It has been restored several times over the years.

3 Memorial Getúlio Vargas
MAP X6 ■ Praça Luís de Camões, Glória ■ (21) 2245 7577 ■ Basement museum: open 10am–5pm Tue–Sun

Brazil's authoritarian president lived in Rio for almost 30 years. These 50-ft (15-m) tall tapering marble columns sitting in an algae-filled pond commemorate him.

Boats moored in Marina da Glória

4 Marina da Glória
MAP X6 ■ Glória

Boats leave from this harbor for tours around Guanabara Bay. Cruises usually take about four hours.

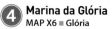

Castelinho do Flamengo

5 Castelinho do Flamengo
MAP H3 ■ Praia do Flamengo 158, Flamengo ■ (21) 2205 0655 ■ Open 10am–8pm Tue–Sat, 10am–6pm Sun

This odd-looking building houses a concert hall and arts center.

6 Parque do Flamengo
MAP H3 ■ Flamengo

Roberto Burle Marx landscaped these extensive gardens. There are wonderful views of the Sugar Loaf.

7 Casa de Arte e Cultura Julieta de Serpa
MAP H3 ■ Praia do Flamengo 340, Flamengo ■ (21) 2551 1278 ■ www.julietadeserpa.com.br

This Art Nouveau building houses a series of restaurants, bars, and exhibition spaces.

8 Oi Futuro Flamengo
MAP H3 ■ Rua Dois de Dezembro 63, Flamengo ■ (21) 3131 3060 ■ www.oifuturo.org.br/cultura/oi-futuro-flamengo

Exhibitions at this ambitious cultural center combine the diverse fields of art, science, and technology, with hands-on displays.

9 Praia Vermelha
MAP J4 ■ Urca

Located between the base of Morro da Urca and Morro da Babilônia, this is home to two university campuses and a few military buildings.

10 Fortaleza de São João
MAP J4 ■ Av João Luís Alves, Urca ■ (21) 2543 3323 ■ Open 9am–4pm Mon–Thu, 9am–noon Fri ■ Adm

Estacio de Sá (see p59) founded this fort in 1565. Only a Baroque gate of the original structure remains.

Places to Eat

PRICE CATEGORIES
For a three-course meal for one with half
a bottle of wine, taxes, and extra charges.
Prices quoted in US dollars.

$ under $25 $$ $25–$50 $$$ over $50

1 Alcaparra
MAP H3 ■ Praia do Flamengo
150, Flamengo ■ (21) 2558 3937
■ $$$

At this Portuguese-Italian restaurant,
the risottos are popular, the desserts
plentiful, and the wine list decent.

2 Laguiole
MAP X4 ■ Av Infante Dom
Henrique 85 ■ (21) 2517 3129 ■ Open
noon–5pm Mon–Fri ■ $$$

Adventurous contemporary cuisine is
the specialty at this restaurant in the
Museu de Arte Moderna (see p39).

3 Café Lamas
MAP H3 ■ Rua Marques de
Abrantes 18, Flamengo ■ (21) 2556
0799 ■ $$

This street-corner snack bar has
been serving steak and chips,
bacalhau (salted cod), crème
caramels, and juices since 1874.

4 Barracuda
MAP K6 ■ Av Infante Dom
Henrique, Marina da Glória, Glória
■ (21) 2265 3346 ■ $$$

Grilled and fried seafood are house
specialties at this fish restaurant.

5 Porcão Rio's
MAP H3 ■ Av Infante Dom
Henrique s/n, Flamengo ■ (21) 3461
9020 ■ $$$

One of Rio's best *churrascaria* (steak
houses); come with an empty stom-
ach for a memorable meal.

6 Casa da Suíça
MAP W5 ■ Rua Cândido
Mendes 157, Glória ■ (21) 2252 5182
■ $$$

A Swiss restaurant that has served
fondue to *Cariocas* for 50 years.

7 Bon Vivant Bistrô e Delicatessen
MAP R1 ■ Rua Voluntários da Pátria
46, Botafogo ■ (21) 2537 2857
■ Open for dinner daily ■ $$

This is a great bistro and
delicatessen in the lower area of
Botafogo. It serves delicious snacks
and local delicacies.

8 Círculo Militar
MAP J4 ■ Praca General
Tibúrcio, Urca ■ (21) 2295-3397 ■ $$

A no-frills but good-value *por kilo*
restaurant in a great location at the
foot of Pão de Açúcar.

Homely interior of Irajá

9 Irajá
MAP G4 ■ Rua Conde de Irajá
109, Botafogo ■ (21) 2246 1395 ■ $$$

With a homely setting in a colonial
mansion, Irajá has been highly
awarded for its adventurous
contemporary cuisine.

10 Miam Miam
MAP R1 ■ Rua General Góes
Monteiro 34, Botafogo ■ (21) 2244
0125 ■ $$$

Light, flavorsome Mediterranean food
is served in this atmospheric brick-
lined restaurant and mini-lounge bar.

See map on p70 ←

🔟 Lagoa, Gávea, and Jardim Botânico

These prosperous, upper-middle-class neighborhoods lie around Lagoa Rodrigo de Freitas, between Ipanema and Leblon, and Corcovado. They are the evening haunts of Rio's rich and fashionable, and the numerous clubs, bars, and restaurants that fill the streets are always busy. Nightlife is at its wildest in Gávea, where the *botecos* around Praça Santos Dumont are particularly lively toward the weekends. During the day, shady parks and tropical gardens tempt visitors away from the beach.

Orchid, Jardim Botânico

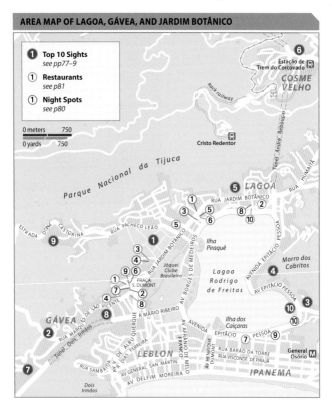

AREA MAP OF LAGOA, GÁVEA, AND JARDIM BOTÂNICO

1 Top 10 Sights
see pp77–9

1 Restaurants
see p81

1 Night Spots
see p80

0 meters 750
0 yards 750

Mural at the Instituto Moreira Salles

1 Jardim Botânico

There are 140 ha (348 acres) of broad, palm-tree-lined avenues, shady paths, and lawns dotted with classical fountains in these beautiful botanical gardens. Many of the trees here – like the *pau brasil*, for which the country was named – are threatened with extinction in the wild. Their branches and fruits and the tropical flowers that fill the garden attract birds and animals from the nearby Floresta da Tijuca. Allow at least three hours for a visit and come at the beginning of the day or after 3pm, when the temperatures are cooler *(see pp24–5)*.

Palm-lined walkway, Jardim Botânico

2 Instituto Moreira Salles

MAP D6 ▪ Rua Marquês de São Vicente 476, Gávea ▪ (21) 3284 7400 ▪ Open 11am–8pm Tue–Sun ▪ www.ims.uol.com.br

This attractive 19th-century house is set in lush grounds landscaped by Roberto Burle Marx, one of the most important landscape architects of the 20th century. The colorful murals on the patio are the work of the famous Brazilian painter Cândido Portinari *(see p21)*. The building is now an exhibition space and café.

3 Fundação Eva Klabin

MAP F6 ▪ Av Epitácio Pessoa 2480, Lagoa ▪ (21) 3202 8550 ▪ www.evaklabin.org.br ▪ Open Tue–Sun 2pm–6pm ▪ Adm

This nationally important private collection contains 2,000 works of art spanning four millennia – from ancient Egyptian sculptures to Impressionist landscapes. The museum is housed in the early 20th-century former home of Klabin, whose possessions and furniture are also meticulously displayed.

4 Parque da Catacumba

MAP N4 ▪ Av Epitácio Pessoa 3,000 ▪ (21) 2247 9949 ▪ Open 8am–6pm daily ▪ www.lagoaaventuras.com.br

Sculptures by Brazilian artists including Bruno Giorgi and Alfredo Ceschiatti dot this wooded park opposite the Lagoa. A 427-ft- (130-m-) high lookout offers great views.

Corcovado looming over Parque Lage

⑤ Parque Lage

MAP M2 ■ Rua Jardim Botânico 414, Jardim Botânico ■ (21) 3257 1800 ■ Open 8am–5pm daily (to 6pm in summer)

An imposing, early-20th-century mansion, housing the School of Visual Art and fronted by Neo-Classical fountains, dominates this park. The house and gardens were designed by Englishman John Tyndale for a wealthy *Carioca* industrialist. The mansion's atrium now houses an arty café. Trails lead from the park to the summit of Corcovado and require a guide.

⑥ Largo do Boticário

MAP G3 ■ Rua Cosme Velho 822, Cosme Velho

This lovely square takes its name from Joaquim Luiz da Silva Souto, who was the pharmacist (*boticário*) to the royal family and lived here from 1831. The enclave boasts colonial-style buildings dating from the 1920s (some with

FAVELAS

Most *Cariocas* live in slum cities – areas of poor-quality housing with little sanitation (**below**). Although most *favelas* are home to law-abiding people, many are plagued by gang violence. These communities have a rich cultural heritage – *samba*, Brazilian soccer, and Carnaval all began here. Only ever visit *favelas* on a guided tour.

picturesque *azulejos* – Portuguese tiles), cobbled streets, and a fountain. The square lies close to the Trem do Corcovado funicular station in Cosme Velho, and can be accessed through the Rebouças tunnel. It is worth visiting en route to the famous statue of Cristo Redentor (see p12).

⑦ Rocinha Favela

MAP D6

The largest *favela* in Latin America takes its name from the little farm, or *rocinha*, that once stood on its now heavily urbanized hills teeming with some 150,000 people. The community here is served by its own local shops, TV and radio stations, restaurants, and bars.

Largo do Boticário

8 Planetário

MAP K4 ▪ Rua Vice-Governador Rubens Berardo 100, Gávea ▪ (21) 2274 0046 ▪ Open 9am–5pm Tue–Fri (3–5pm Dec–Mar), 2:30–5pm Sat & Sun; telescopes 6:30pm Wed (7:30am–9:30pm Dec–Mar) ▪ Adm ▪ www.planetariodorio.com.br

Gávea's stellar attraction, this complex features a museum of the universe, ultra-modern domes that can project thousands of stars onto their walls, and a viewing area, which offers stargazing sessions through powerful telescopes.

9 Horto Florestal

MAP L3 ▪ Rua Pacheco Leão 2040, Jardim Botânico ▪ (21) 3875 6211 ▪ Open 9–11am & 2–4pm Mon–Fri

This arboretum, located next to the Jardim Botânico, cultivates some 500 kinds of tropical trees, many of which are rare species from the Atlantic coastal rain forest. Seedlings are sold, along with advice on planting, to encourage reforestation.

10 Parque do Cantagalo

MAP P4 ▪ Parque do Cantagalo, Av Epitácio Pessoa s/n, Lagoa

This circular park winds around Lagoa Rodrigo de Freitas. There is a running track situated close to the water here, as well as cafés and bars where locals come to relax in the shade. Swan-shaped pedal boats and kayaks can be hired at the lake.

Parque do Cantagalo

A DAY IN RIO'S PARKS AND GARDENS

▶ MORNING

Start the day with a stroll around **Jardim Botânico** *(see pp24–5)*. Try to arrive as close to 8am as possible and with binoculars in hand for the best chance to spot brilliantly colored birds like tanagers, cotingas, and numerous hummingbirds, as well as small mammals like *paca* and *agouti*. There is a kiosk at the entrance that gives out free maps of the gardens in a variety of languages, explaining where the important sights, including glasshouses such as the **Orquidarium**, are situated. At about 11am, as the morning heats up, consider taking a helicopter flight over **Corcovado** *(see pp12–13)* from the helipad just to the south of **Jardim Botânico**. The views of **Cristo Redentor** *(see p12)* from the air are amazing.

AFTERNOON

Have lunch at one of the many kiosks overlooking **Lagoa Rodrigo de Freitas** on the eastern shore of the lake, which is in close proximity to the **Parque da Catacumba** *(see p77)*. Drink plenty of juice or water and walk across Avenida Epitácio Pessoa for a 40-minute hike through the park, to the 427-ft-(130-m-) high lookout point at the Mirante do Sacopã. If there are no guards around, then be vigilant in the park or walk in a group. Head to **Parque Lage** by taxi for a pony ride or another light walk in the rain forest. Finish the afternoon with tea and biscuits in the mansion's café.

See map on p76 ⬅

Night Spots

Diners at Hipódromo Up

1 Bar Jóia Carioca
MAP M3 ■ Rua Jardim Botânico 594 ■ (21) 2539 5613

This unpretentious and informal little street-corner bar attracts an eclectic young and local crowd at weekends and in the evenings.

2 Garota da Gávea
MAP K4 ■ Praça Santos Dumont 148 ■ (21) 2274 2347

On weekends, scores of people gather at this lively bar, just off Praça Santos Dumont, for *petiscos* (tapas) and drinks.

3 Belmonte
MAP N2 ■ Rua Jardim Botânico 617 ■ (21) 2239 1649

Bakeries like Belmonte play an integral part in Brazil's nightlife, serving *empadas* (little stuffed filo pies) at all hours.

4 Espaço Tom Jobim
MAP E5 ■ Rua Jardim Botânico ■ www.jbrj.gov.br

This arts center in the Jardim Botânico, named after one of the founders of Bossa Nova, offers a diverse program of live concerts, shows, and art exhibitions.

5 Kiosque do Português
MAP F5 ■ Rua Jardim Botânico 585 ■ (21) 2239 9936

This bar, with stunning views over Lagoa Rodrigo de Freitas, has won awards for its fruity cocktails.

6 Hipódromo Up
MAP K4 ■ Praça Santos Dumont 108 ■ (21) 2274 9720

Filled with young *Cariocas* who come to mingle, this is a wonderful spot to meet the locals.

7 Marquês da Gávea
MAP E5 ■ Praça Santos Dumont 126, Gávea ■ (21) 3114 0780

This local sports *boteco* is decorated from top to bottom with soccer memorabilia, and is particularly heaving on match days, serving chilled beer and pub food.

8 La Carioca Cevicheria
MAP F6 ■ Rua Maria Angélica 113A, Lagoa ■ (21) 2226 8821

One of Rio's few Peruvian eateries, this restaurant dishes up authentic *ceviche*, marinated fish, as well as pisco sours and other fiery cocktails.

9 Bar Lagoa
MAP P5 ■ Av Epitácio Pessoa 1674 ■ (21) 2523 1135

Petiscos and cocktails are on offer at Bar Lagoa, one of the oldest *botecos* in the area. There is also live music on most Fridays and weekends.

10 Palaphita Kitch
MAP P5 ■ Av Epitácio Pessoa, kiosk 20 ■ (21) 2227 0837

The rustic log tables and chairs strewn under mock-Bedouin awnings and the strong *caipirinhas* make this a favorite *Carioca* haunt.

Restaurants

PRICE CATEGORIES
For a three-course meal for one with half a bottle of wine, taxes, and extra charges. Prices are quoted in US dollars.

$ under $25 $$ $25–$50 $$$ over $50

 Guimas
MAP K4 ▪ Rua José Roberto Macedo Soares 5 ▪ (21) 2259 7996 ▪ $$

Carioca celebrities lunch at this rustic restaurant, serving traditional Portuguese and Brazilian cuisine.

2 CT Trattorie
MAP N2 ▪ Av Alexandre Ferreira 66 ▪ (21) 2266 0838 ▪ $$

Opened by Olympe's *(see p50)* chef Claude Troisgros, this French bistro has an affordable lunch buffet and classic French dishes.

3 La Bicyclette
MAP F5 ▪ Rua Jardim Botânico 1008 ▪ (21) 3594 2589 ▪ $$

Located inside the Jardim Botânico, this French bakery offers brunches, snacks, and hearty lunches.

4 Árabe da Gávea
MAP K4 ▪ Rua Marquês de São Vicente 52, Shopping da Gávea ▪ (21) 2294 3528 ▪ $$

One of Rio's best Arabic restaurants bustles after dark.

5 Volta
MAP E5 ▪ Rua Visconde de Carandaí 5 ▪ (21) 3204 5406 ▪ $$

Specialties at this contemporary Brazilian restaurant include grilled ray with lentils and crispy onion, and Spanish-style *churros* (fried choux pastry) with *dulce de leche*.

6 Quadrifoglio
MAP M3 ▪ Rua JJ Seabra 19 ▪ (21) 2294 1433 ▪ $

This chic Italian eatery is divided into a series of dining rooms, each with its own unique atmosphere.

7 Pomodorino
MAP N5 ▪ Av Epitácio Pessoa 1104 ▪ (21) 3813 2622 ▪ $$

Run by the owners of highly rated Artigiano, Pomodorino serves sublime Italian dishes and has a great selection of good-value wines.

8 Bacalhau do Rei
MAP K4 ▪ Rua Marquês de São Vicente 11A ▪ (21) 2239 8945 ▪ $$

This family restaurant is frequented by Rio's Portuguese community and gets particularly busy on Sundays.

9 Braseiro da Gávea
MAP K4 ▪ Praça Santos Dumont 116 ▪ (21) 2239 7494 ▪ $$

Serving variations on the traditional Brazilian meal, this restaurant is a popular meeting point for locals.

10 Mr Lam
MAP N2 ▪ Rua Maria Angélica 21 ▪ (21) 2286 6661 ▪ $$$

With a partial view of Corcovado *(see pp12–13)*, this vast, glass-walled Chinese restaurant is a stomping ground for affluent *Cariocas*.

Old-world ambience at Guimas

🔟 Santa Teresa and Lapa

Escadaria Selarón detail

Charming architecture, cobbled streets, and a sense of community spirit give Santa Teresa an identity of its own. This unique character coupled with the superb panoramas have made the area popular with both tourists and locals. Brilliantly colored mosaic steps connect Santa Teresa with its neighbor, Lapa, which was destitute until a renaissance began in the late 1990s. Inspired by the return of the Circo Voador club, the area was transformed into the city's hottest night spot.

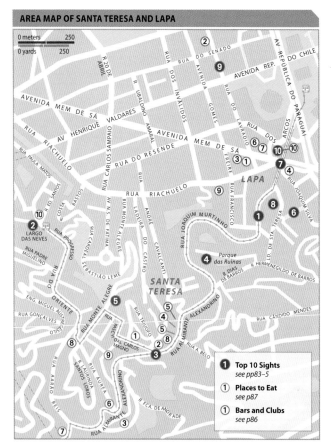

AREA MAP OF SANTA TERESA AND LAPA

❶	Top 10 Sights see pp83–5
①	Places to Eat see p87
①	Bars and Clubs see p86

A tram in Santa Teresa

1 Tram Rides
MAP V5 ■ Tram terminal: Rua Lélio Gama ■ (21) 2240 5709 ■ Trams run 6am–10pm daily ■ Adm

Trams are the best way to reach Santa Teresa from Centro. They jerk their way from a station next to the Catedral Metropolitana de São Sebastião *(see p66)*, across the Arcos da Lapa, and up the steep streets of Santa Teresa. The journey takes about 20 minutes and the trams are packed with colorful characters of all ages and backgrounds, many of whom are left precariously hanging on to the bars that run along the side of the tram.

2 Largo das Neves
MAP T5

The smaller of Santa Teresa's two *praças* (town squares) is a great place to sit and watch the world go by. There are several *botecos* and restaurants here serving cold beer, pizza, and seafood dishes. It is the starting point of the Santa Teresa Carnaval parade *(see p58)*.

3 Largo dos Guimarães
MAP V6

Many of Santa Teresa's best restaurants are clustered around this square, including Espírito Santa *(see p86)* and Bar do Mineiro *(see p87)*. The area also features arts and crafts shops, and nearby, on Rua do Aqueducto, is a little yellow booth shaped like a tram, where the model trams found in many of Santa Teresa's restaurants are made by artisan Getúlio Damato.

Parque das Ruínas

4 Chácara do Céu
MAP V5 ■ Rua Murtinho Nobre 93, Santa Teresa ■ (21) 3970 1126 ■ Open noon–5pm Wed–Mon ■ Adm (free on Wed) ■ www.museuscastromaya.com.br

The Chácara mansion, which has fantastic views over the city center, houses an exquisite museum featuring European and Asian art and antiques, as well as modern Brazilian works. Next door is the Parque das Ruínas *(see p48)* – a park containing the shell of another colonial mansion.

Largo dos Guimarães

The 18th-century aqueduct turned viaduct, Arcos da Lapa

5 Museu Casa Benjamin Constant

MAP U5 ▪ Rua Monte Alegre 255, Santa Teresa ▪ (21) 2509 1248 ▪ Open 10am–5pm Wed–Fri, 1–5pm Sat & Sun ▪ Adm

This is the former home of Benjamin Constant, a political philosopher who led the republican movement and formulated key political ideas including the national motto, *Ordem e Progresso* (Order and Progress). The museum contains many personal items and offers great views.

6 Escadaria Selarón

MAP W5 ▪ Rua Joaquim Silva, Lapa

These steps link Rua Joaquim Silva in Lapa with Ladeira de Santa Teresa in Santa Teresa. Their official name is the Escadaria do Convento de Santa Teresa but locals refer to them as the Escadaria Selarón – in homage to the Chilean artist, Jorge Selarón, who decorated them with colored and mirrored mosaic tiles.

7 Arcos da Lapa

MAP W4

Lapa is dominated by this aqueduct passing over Avenida Mem de Sá, which was built in 1724 to transport water from the Santa Teresa forest to the public drinking fountain near Largo da Carioca. Trams now run across the arches to and from Santa Teresa; lively bars and arts centers draw crowds to the adjoining square.

8 Convento de Santa Teresa

MAP W5 ▪ Ladeira de Santa Teresa 52, Santa Teresa ▪ (21) 2224 1040 ▪ Open 7am–5pm Mon–Fri (to 4pm Sat & Sun)

The Santa Teresa district is named for this austere 18th-century convent, which was built in honor of St. Teresa – founder of the Discalced Carmelite order of the Catholic Church and disciple and friend of St. John of the Cross. When it was completed in 1757, this became the first female convent in Brazil. Although much of the convent is

The colorful Escadaria Selarón

RONNIE BIGGS

Ronnie Biggs was a member of the gang that carried out "The Great Train Robbery" in England in 1963. He fled to Rio, settling in Santa Teresa. Biggs could not be extradited as he had fathered a Brazilian child. He returned voluntarily to the UK in 2001 because of ill health. He was arrested, but then released from prison on compassionate grounds in 2009 and died in 2013.

closed to visitors, there is a small museum as well as access to the very spot where St. Teresa was born and the little garden where she used to play as a child.

9 Feira do Rio Antigo
MAP W4

On the first Saturday of each month, there is a lively antiques and bric-a-brac fair on Rua do Lavradio, northeast of Arcos da Lapa. The streets fill up with old-fashioned, second-hand furniture and house-hold items, as well as people dancing to live bands playing *samba* and, unusually for Rio, tango.

Feira do Rio Antigo

10 Circo Voador
MAP W4 ▪ Rua dos Arcos s/n, Lapa ▪ (21) 2533 0354
▪ www.circovoador.com.br

This concert arena and its coterie of musicians and artists have revitalized Lapa, which was once dangerous and decrepit. Shows at the Circo attracted visitors and brought new life to old *samba* clubs, encouraging new clubs to open. Some of Rio's best acts, including Seu Jorge, began here. The Circo is a great place to check out Rio's cutting-edge live talent.

TWO NIGHTS OF MUSIC IN LAPA

▶ FRIDAY

There is nowhere better to get acquainted with the bewildering diversity of Brazilian musical styles than in Lapa on a Friday night. Begin at around 8pm with an ice-cold *chopp* beer in **Belmonte Lapa** (*see p68*) on Avenida Mem de Sá (where there is a street party on Friday and Saturday nights). *Choro*, which was popular in Rio before *samba*, can be heard live at **Carioca da Gema** (*see p86*), which is also on Avenida Mem da Sá. This club has a great pizza restaurant. At about 10pm, leave **Carioca da Gema** for some *gafieira* or ballroom *samba*, played by a big band fronted by a single singer. *Gafieira* is best heard some 300 ft (91 m) away at the **Clube dos Democraticos** (*see p86*). Be prepared to dance and be danced with. After this, sample some live *samba* at the nearby **Rio Scenarium** (*see p86*) – the former is small and intimate, the latter larger with a Bohemian atmosphere. Both play famous *samba* standards.

SATURDAY

If Friday has not left you exhausted, come back on Saturday evening to the **Circo Voador** for more Rio funk, or dance around Largo da Lapa to some northeastern Brazilian *forró* played on accordion, triangle, and *surdo* drum. Other options include *bossa nova* electronica at **Espírito Santa** (*see p86*), or more from the endless list of Brazilian musical styles.

See map on p82 ←

Bars and Clubs

Live music at Carioca da Gema

1 Carioca da Gema
MAP W4 ■ Av Mem de Sá 79, Lapa ■ (21) 2221 0043

This is one of Rio's best *samba* and *choro* bars. Upstairs is a pizza restaurant, where different live acts play sets late into the night.

2 Rio Scenarium
MAP V3 ■ Rua do Lavradio 20, Lapa ■ (21) 3147 9000

One of the larger *samba* clubs in Rio, this popular venue hosts live bands on the ground floor and has bars and dance floors on the upper levels.

3 Sacrilégio
MAP V4 ■ Av Mem de Sá 81, Lapa ■ (21) 3970 1461

Excellent live acts play in this *samba* club located in an 18th-century house decorated in green and white.

4 Bar Semente
MAP W4 ■ Rua Evaristo da Veiga 149, Lapa ■ (21) 2507 5188

This small, convivial spot hosts outstanding music performances. It is visited by famous musicians who are also invited to play a song or two.

5 Espírito Santa
MAP V6 ■ Rua Almirante Alexandrino 264, Santa Teresa ■ (21) 2507 4840

Upstairs is a restaurant decorated with modern art and a terrace that offers wonderful views of the city. Downstairs is a club that plays funk and Brazilian groove on Fridays.

6 Choperia Brazooka
MAP W4 ■ Ave Mem de Sá 70, Lapa ■ (21) 2224 3236

Pounding with music from live rock bands, this huge venue has three bars over four floors and is a popular spot with loyal Lapa locals.

7 Teatro Odisséia
MAP W4 ■ Av Mem de Sá 66, Lapa ■ (21) 2226 9691

This converted three-storey ware-house rocks to the sound of live bands at weekends, and also puts on art exhibitions and plays.

8 Armazém São Thiago
MAP U6 ■ Rua Áurea 26, Santa Teresa ■ (21) 2232 0822

Also known as Bar do Gomes, this Santa Teresa bar buzzes with charm and character, from the cabinet-lined walls to the loyal clientele.

9 Clube dos Democráticos
MAP V5 ■ Rua da Riachuelo 91, Lapa ■ (21) 2252 4611

This 19th-century ballroom has a stage large enough for big *samba* bands with up to 20 members, and hosts ballroom *samba* and *gafieira* bands on weekends.

Clube dos Democráticos

10 Circo Voador
The best of Rio's emerging funk acts play alongside established stars in Lapa's principal concert hall. Many well-known singers got their big break here *(see p85)*.

Places to Eat

1 **Bar do Mineiro**
MAP V6 ▪ Rua Paschoal Carlos Magno 99 ▪ (21) 2221 9227 ▪ $

The tasty snacks here include *bolinhos de bacalhau* (salted cod fritters) and *feijoada* (bean and meat stew).

2 **Sobrenatural**
MAP V6 ▪ Av Almirante Alexandrino 432, Santa Teresa ▪ (21) 2224 1003 ▪ $$

Santa Teresa's most popular eatery serves excellent seafood. There is live *samba* and *choro* on Fridays.

Outdoor dining at Aprazível

3 **Aprazível**
MAP U6 ▪ Rua Aprazivel 62, Santa Teresa ▪ (21) 2508 9174 ▪ $$$

This open-air restaurant specializes in seafood and traditional dishes like *galinhada caipira* (chicken risotto with *mineiro* sausage, chicory, and beans).

4 **Adega do Pimenta**
MAP V6 ▪ Rua Almirante Alexandrino 296, Santa Teresa ▪ (21) 2224 7554 ▪ $$

Enjoy the creative dishes on offer here, including roast rabbit with curried cauliflower.

5 **Bar do Arnaudo**
MAP U6 ▪ Rua Almirante Alexandrino 316, Santa Teresa ▪ (21) 2146 6704 ▪ $

This cozy, long-standing *boteco* serves up *petiscos* (tapas) and northeastern mains, including Bahian *moquecas* (fish stew) and *carne do sol* (salted beef).

6 **Alda Maria**
MAP U6 ▪ Rua Almirante Alexandrino 1116, Santa Teresa ▪ (21) 2232 1320 ▪ $

This local bakery serves Portuguese cakes and pastries, including *pasteis de nata* (custard tarts). It has good coffee and a cozy atmosphere.

7 **Mike's Haus**
MAP V6 ▪ Rua Almirante Alexandrino 1458A, Santa Teresa ▪ (21) 2509 5248 ▪ $$

Feast on delicious *petiscos* and a range of German sausages, including Kalbsbratwurst and Nuernberger, at this popular restaurant. Sample beer imported from Germany.

8 **Sansushi**
MAP V6 ▪ Rua Almirante Alexandrino 382, Santa Teresa ▪ (21) 2252 0581 ▪ $$

Diners sit in small wooden booths in one of Rio's most traditional Japanese restaurants to eat sushi and noodles.

9 **Térèze**
MAP U6 ▪ Rua Felício dos Santos, Santa Teresa ▪ (21) 3380 0220 ▪ $$$

The elegant restaurant in the Hotel Santa Teresa is pricey but highly rated.

10 **Goya Beira**
MAP U5 ▪ Largo das Neves 13, Santa Teresa ▪ (21) 2232 5751 ▪ $

A busy little *boteco* with a glass-fronted bar. *Cariocas* come here to enjoy the cold *chopp* (draft beer) and *petiscos* after work.

Following pages Elaborate Carnaval float in the Sambódromo

🔟 Copacabana, Ipanema, and Leblon

Rio's association with the beach is strong, courtesy of the stunning Copacabana and Ipanema beaches, whose sweeping sands look south across the Atlantic. These beaches are backed by a series of bustling neighborhoods: Copacabana and Leme lie behind Copacabana beach, and Ipanema beach backs onto Aproador, Leblon, and Ipanema. Arpoador, Ipanema, and Leblon attract an exclusive crowd, while Copacabana and Leme beaches are somewhat tawdry.

Gay Pride flags along a section of Ipanema beach

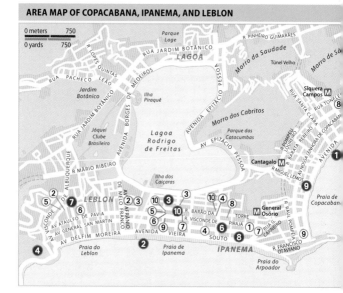

AREA MAP OF COPACABANA, IPANEMA, AND LEBLON

1 Praia de Copacabana

Rio's most famous stretch of beach is a vast 4-mile (6.4-km) sweep of powder-fine sand along the shores of the Atlantic. It is backed by a broad, four-lane avenue studded with Art Deco apartment blocks and towering hotels, the most famous being the Copacabana Palace (see p112). The avenue is lined on either side by wave-patterned mosaic pavements and has cafés and juice kiosks along its length (see pp30–31).

2 Ipanema and Leblon Beachlife

Ipanema and Leblon beaches are where fashion-conscious and gay and lesbian Rio comes to lounge and relax in the sun. An afternoon here is an essential experience. Bring as little as possible. Sun-shades, deck chairs, snacks, and drinks are readily available on the beach (see pp32–3).

3 Ipanema's Fashionable Streets

MAP M5 ■ Ipanema

Ruas Garcia d'Avila, Visconde de Pirajá, and Nascimento da Silva in

Ipanema and Leblon beaches

Ipanema are home to the most exclusive designer boutiques, jewelry shops, and cafés in Rio (see pp94–5). Top Brazilian brands like Lenny and Antonio Bernardo vie for street space with international names such as Louis Vuitton. And although it is possible to find bargains in shops like Toulon (see p94), prices are above average.

4 Dois Irmãos

MAP K6 ■ Leblon

The "Two Brothers" – twin peaks that tower over Leblon – look particularly beautiful at dusk, when the sky turns pink and the waves are bottle-green. A lookout from Dois Irmãos boasting great views over Leblon and Ipanema is reachable from the beach end of Avenida Ataúlfo de Paiva in Leblon.

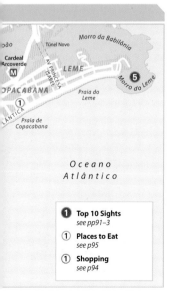

Dois Irmãos tower over Leblon

Morro do Leme, at the northern end of Praia de Copacabana

5 Morro do Leme
This boulder hill watches over Copacabana from the Leme end of the beach. It is a great spot to visit on a Sunday afternoon, when lively *samba* bands play near the seafood kiosks. Paths and a climbing trail wind around the rock, but these are not safe without a tour guide – assaults and robberies are not uncommon here *(see p31)*.

6 Garota de Ipanema
MAP N5 ▪ Rua Vinicius de Moraes 49, Ipanema ▪ (21) 2523 3787
In the early 1960s, the poet Vinícius de Moraes and his composer friend Antônio Carlos Jobim met regularly in this little bar. Inspired by a beautiful girl who used to pass by, the duo wrote the song *Garota de Ipanema*. When Brazilian guitarist João Gilberto, his wife Astrud, and

US jazz saxophonist Stan Getz recorded it in English as *The Girl from Ipanema*, they popularized *bossa nova*.

7 Rua Dias Ferreira
MAP K5
Some of the best restaurants and bars in the city line this upmarket, chic street at the end of Leblon. It is worth heading down here for an evening stroll before deciding where to dine. Restaurants range from family-run businesses, such as Celeiro *(see p95)*, to the likes of Zuka *(see p50)* and Sushi Leblon *(see p95)*, which were founded by chefs who previously worked in New York or London. Cuisines range from French to modern Brazilian, Japanese, *churrascaria (see p110)*, and Asian-South American fusion. Dress codes are informal.

8 Casa de Cultura Laura Alvim
MAP P6 ▪ Av Vieira Souto 176, Ipanema ▪ (21) 2332 2016 ▪ Open 1–9pm Tue–Sun
Patron of the arts Laura Agostini Alvim founded this arts center in her old house in Ipanema. It exhibits artworks from Alvim's friends and admirers, including Angelo de Aquino, Paulo Roberto Leal, Roberto Moriconi, and Rubens Guerchman, and hosts visiting exhibitions, small concerts, and book launches. It also has an arts cinema and theater.

Garota de Ipanema

BOSSA NOVA

Bossa nova is gentrified *samba*, sung in a spoken or whispered voice. Born in the 1950s, when Moraes, Jobim, and Gilberto began composing songs together, *bossa nova* became internationally famous with Camus' 1960 film *Black Orpheus*. It can be heard at Toca do Vinícius *(see p94)* on Sunday afternoons.

⑨ Museu da Imagem e da Som

MAP Q5 ▪ Av Atlântica 3432 ▪ www.mis.rj.gov.br

The futuristic new museum of Image and Sound dominates Avenida Atlântica – its zigzag lines and flower-filled terraces break up the ranks of tower blocks that line the avenue along Copacabana Beach. The museum collections offer a similarly bold display of cutting-edge technology, with exhibits focusing on Rio de Janeiro's incomparable heritage of music and dance.

Jewelry at Museu H. Stern

⑩ Museu H. Stern

MAP M5 ▪ Rua Garcia d'Avila 113, Ipanema ▪ (21) 2106 0000

The workshops in Brazil's largest upmarket jewelry chain are open to tour groups, who are encouraged to watch stones as they are cut, polished, and set. The guides are knowledgeable about the processes, so be sure to ask questions. Visits finish at the museum shop, where a series of carefully lit display cases show pieces from H. Stern's latest jewelry catalog.

A DAY AT THE BEACH

Lagoa Rodrigo de Freitas

Rua Dias Ferreira

Rua Garcia d'Avila

Garota de Ipanema

LEBLON

PANEMA

Praia do Leblon

Praia de Ipanema

▶ MORNING

Pack your beach bag with the minimum and bring a moderate amount of cash. To blend in with the locals, women should slip on a *tanga* (bikini) and a *canga* (sarong). Men should dress in board shorts over a *sunga* (rectangular-cut speedos), and wear a loose T-shirt. Finish the look with sunglasses and *chinelos* (flip-flops) – all available in shops at Ipanema and Copacabana. Put a novel and sun cream (factor 30) in your beach bag and head to one of the many juice kiosks in **Ipanema** and **Copacabana** for a coconut water or an *açai* [see p41]. Arrive on the beach before 9:30am to sunbathe. You will not overheat as the water here is surprisingly chilly. Swim at **Leblon**, which has the cleanest water. Areas with strong currents are always flagged.

AFTERNOON

Beachwear is acceptable everywhere except in formal lunchtime restaurants. Have a relaxed meal, a coffee, and browse in the shops along **Rua Garcia d'Avila**. From 3:30pm people begin surfing, cycling, and playing beach volleyball or soccer. Mingle with the locals or just jog along the warm sand. Romantic strolls along the waterfront are wonderful in the afternoon and beach massages are popular as the air gets cool. After sunset, head to a *boteco* like **Garota de Ipanema** in Ipanema for an ice-cold *chopp* (draft beer). Return to the hotel to change before going out to one of the many restaurants along **Rua Dias Ferreira**.

See map on pp90–91

Shopping

1 **Feira Hippie Market**
MAP P5 ■ Praça General Osório
■ Open 7am–7pm Sun

Praça General Osório's Sunday bric-a-brac market has stalls selling crafts, household items, and clothes.

2 **Shopping Leblon**
MAP L5 ■ Av Afrânio de Melo Franco 290 ■ (21) 2430 5122

This mall on Leblon's largest shopping street houses a large number of shops of both local and international brands. It also has restaurants, a multiplex, and children's play area.

3 **Kiehl's**
MAP L5 ■ Av Afrânio de Melo Franco 290 ■ (21) 2239 0049

This branch of the natural cosmetics and pharmacy chain offers a range of beauty products that are free from colorings and preservatives, and come in biodegradable containers.

4 **Toca do Vinícius**
MAP N5 ■ Rua Vinícius de Moraes 129, Ipanema ■ (21) 2247 5227

Choro, *samba*, and *bossa nova* fill the shelves of this shop. You can listen to CDs before deciding what to buy.

5 **Toulon**
MAP M5 ■ Rua Visconde de Pirajá 540, Ipanema ■ (21) 2239 2195

Head to Toulon to stock up on jeans, jackets, shirts, and swimwear.

6 **Folic**
MAP M5 ■ Loja B, Rua Visconde de Pirajá 540, Ipanema ■ (21) 2512 9323

This fashionable women's label with over 50 stores throughout Brazil sells clothes made from fine fabrics.

7 **Gilson Martins**
MAP N5 ■ Rua Visconde de Pirajá 462B ■ (21) 2227 6178

This shop's range of bright, funky bags are crafted from a variety of materials, such as leather, plastic, and vinyl, and come in a variety of *Carioca* shapes – from a soccer ball to the Sugar Loaf.

8 **Baratos da Ribeiro**
MAP R3 ■ Rua Barata Ribeiro 354, Copacabana ■ (21) 2256 8634

A shrine for *Carioca* music lovers, this shop stocks more than 15,000 CDs and thousands of second-hand books, many in English.

Funky bags at Gilson Martins

9 **Victor Hugo**
MAP N5 ■ Rua Visconde de Pirajá 507, Ipanema ■ (21) 2259 9699

Brazil's counterpart to Louis Vuitton, Victor Hugo attracts Rio's sophisticated set with its collection of branded wallets, purses, handbags, and personal luggage.

10 **Maria Bonita**
MAP N5 ■ Rua Vinicius de Moraes 149, Ipanema ■ (21) 2523 4093

Known for her tops and famous jersey dresses with wrap fronts and high, elasticated waists, Maria Bonita is popular internationally.

Places to Eat

 Cipriani
MAP R3 ■ Av Atlântica 1702, Copacabana ■ (21) 2545 8747 ■ $$$
The Copacabana Palace's *(see p112) haute cuisine* restaurant is named for the luxurious Cipriani hotel in Venice and features excellent north Italian dishes in an opulent dining room.

2 **Sushi Leblon**
MAP K5 ■ Rua Dias Ferreira 256, Leblon ■ (21) 2512 7830 ■ $$$
Rio's most celebrated Japanese restaurant was the first in the city to experiment with Japanese–Western fusion cuisine.

3 **Alessandro e Frederico Café**
MAP M5 ■ Rua Garcia d'Avila 134D, Ipanema ■ (21) 2521 0828 ■ $$
A favorite with Ipanema's socialites, this restaurant serves tasty salmon in sweet and sour sauce and excellent coffee.

4 **Zazá Bistrô Tropical**
MAP N6 ■ Rua Joana Angélica 40, Ipanema ■ (21) 2247 9101 ■ $$$
This brightly colored bistro, a block from the beach, serves Mediterranean and Eastern food, including Vietnamese rolls.

5 **Celeiro**
MAP K5 ■ Rua Dias Ferreira 199, Leblon ■ (21) 2274 7843 ■ $$
Celeiro serves a broad range of delicious organic salads and light meals, as well as cakes and juices.

Forneria São Sebastião

PRICE CATEGORIES
For a three-course meal for one with half a bottle of wine, taxes, and extra charges. Prices are quoted in US dollars.

$ under $25 $$ $25–$50 $$$ over $50

---

6 **Fellini**
MAP L5 ■ Rua Gen Urquiza 104, Leblon ■ (21) 2511 3600 ■ $$
One of the best buffet restaurants in Leblon, Fellini serves meat and fish dishes, and good vegetarian dishes.

7 **Casa da Feijoada**
MAP P6 ■ Rua Prudente de Morais 10, Ipanema ■ (21) 2247 2776 ■ $$
Enjoy a traditional lunch of the national dish *feijoada*, which is made from black beans, pork, and beef.

8 **New Natural**
MAP N5 ■ Rua Barão da Torre 173, Ipanema ■ (21) 2247 9363 ■ $
This mostly vegetarian and whole foods restaurant offers salads, soups, and soya "meat" casseroles.

9 **Le Pré Catalan**
MAP Q5 ■ Sofitel, Av Atlântica 4240, Copacabana ■ (21) 2525 1160 ■ $$$
Tasty Franco-Brazilian cuisine. The set menu is excellent value.

10 **Forneria São Sebastião**
MAP M5 ■ Rua Aníbal de Mendonça 112, Ipanema ■ (21) 2540 8045 ■ $$
This Italian restaurant specializes in pizzas and burgers in *panini* rolls.

🔟 Western Beaches

Since the 1960s, Rio has been spreading west, boosted by the construction of the Olympic Park on the shore of the revitalized Lagoa de Jacarepaguá. From São Conrado through Barra da Tijuca to Recreio dos Bandeirantes are 12 miles (20 km) of some of the city's most beautiful and unspoilt beaches, with pounding waves drawing the city's top surfers. Lining the area's broad avenues are upscale residential complexes, dozens of shopping malls, and giant arenas. Nevertheless, you can escape the crowds at the pristine wildlife reserves and parks, or several fascinating specialist museums.

Garden statue, Sítio Burle Marx

Parque de Marapendi, surrounding Lagoa de Marapendi

AREA MAP OF WESTERN BEACHES

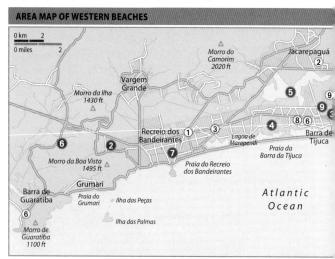

① Barra da Tijuca
MAP B6

Booming Barra da Tijuca is spread along the city's longest beach, whose huge Atlantic breakers make it popular with surfers. With its giant shopping malls, wide avenues, and gated condominiums, Barra looks more like an American neighborhood than a Brazilian one *(see p40)*.

② Museu Casa do Pontal
MAP A6 ▪ Estrada do Pontal 3295, Recreio ▪ (21) 2490 2429 ▪ www.museucasadopontal.com.br ▪ Open 9:30am–5pm Tue–Fri, 10:30am–6pm Sat & Sun

Home to the largest collection of folk art in Brazil, this specialist museum is one of Rio's lesser-known gems. Thousands of delightfully quirky ceramic and wooden figurines are arranged thematically in an airy modern building, covering all aspects of rural and city life; from a football match and a car workshop to a carnaval parade. It even has graphically explicit erotic exhibits in an adults-only section. Plans are afoot to move the museum from its current isolated location to the new Porto Maravilha, in downtown Rio.

Barra da Tijuca from Pedra da Gávea

③ Cidade das Artes
MAP B6 ▪ Av das Américas 5300, Barra da Tijuca ▪ (21) 3325 0102 ▪ www.cidadedasartes.org ▪ Open 10am–6pm Tue–Sun (later during performances)

Barra's huge arts complex was nearly 10 years in the making, finally opening in 2013, by which time its budget had rocketed to R$515 million (US$250 million). Designed by French architect Christian Portzamparc, the angular concrete building houses the 1,800-seat home of the Brazilian Symphony Orchestra, as well as an art gallery, cinemas, shops, and restaurants.

④ Parque de Marapendi
MAP B6 ▪ Av Alfredo Baltazar da Silveira, Recreio dos Bandeirantes ▪ (21) 2497 7088 ▪ Open 8am–5pm Tue–Sun

Bordering the long narrow lagoon that runs parallel to the Praia de Recreio, this wildlife reserve comprises mangroves and *restinga* (sandbanks), home to waterbirds, reptiles, and other native species. Two paths run through the park, one leading to the Lagoa de Marapendi.

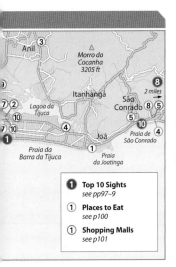

Green waters of Lagoa de Jacarepaguá with Barra da Tijuca behind

⑤ Lagoa de Jacarepaguá
MAP B6 ▪ **Barra da Tijuca**

Lying between Barra da Tijuca and one of Rio's biggest *favelas*, Cidade de Deus, this lagoon is the site of the Rio Olympic Park. A huge replanting project is restoring the shore's neglected borders, with the addition of thousands of mangrove and marsh plants. After 2016, it will be converted into a park, with a sports center, lakeside gardens, and cycle paths, as well as boating amenities.

⑥ Sítio Burle Marx
MAP A6 ▪ **Estrada Roberto Burle Marx 2019, Barra de Guaratiba** ▪ **(21) 2410 1412** ▪ **sitioburlemarx. blogspot.com.br** ▪ **Open 9am–1:30pm Tue–Sat**

These lush landscaped gardens and house were the home of Roberto

BIODIVERSITY

The Mata Atlântica, or Atlantic coastal rain forest, is isolated from other major South American rain forests by the continent's arid interior, and therefore many of this area's diverse plant and animal species exist only here. Today, less than eight percent of the original forest is left and Brazilians are beginning to realize that eco-tourism is crucial for the rain forest's survival.

Burle Marx, Brazilian landscape designer, who was responsible for much of Rio's modern cityscape, including the iconic wavy pavement mosaics along Copacabana Beach (see pp30–31). Tours are available at 9am and 1:30pm by appointment.

⑦ Parque Ecológico Chico Mendes
MAP A6 ▪ **Av Jarbas de Carvalho 679, Recreio dos Bandeirantes** ▪ **(21) 2437 6400** ▪ **Open 8am–5pm Tue–Sun (to 6pm in summer)**

This ecological reserve comprises an area of marshes and *restinga* (sandbanks) typical of this low-lying region. Named for an environ-mentalist murdered in 1988, the park is home to various endangered plants and animals, including the yellow-throated caiman and three-toed sloth. Trails lead to a small lagoon and an observation tower offers good bird-watching and views over the flat landscape.

Landscaped garden, Sítio Burle Marx

8 Parque da Cidade
MAP B6 ■ Estrada Santa Marinha, Gávea ■ (21) 2259 9295 ■ Open 7am–5pm daily (to 6pm in summer)

These hillside gardens, bordering Tijuca National Park, were the estate of the Marquês de São Vicente, a 19th-century politician. His former home is now Rio's city history museum, but the park's lawns and ornamental pond are a peaceful spot for a stroll, with great sea views.

9 Bosque da Barra
MAP B6 ■ Av das Americas 2430, Barra ■ (21) 3325 0302 ■ Open 8am–5pm Tue–Sun

This marshy wildlife reserve lies in the center of Barra, flanked by two of the district's busiest thoroughfares. The park shelters a wide variety of waterbirds and animals, including caiman and capybara, the world's largest rodent. Trails and cycle paths run through the park, which also has a playground, volleyball courts, football pitches, and an outdoor gym.

Praia de São Conrado

10 Praia de São Conrado
MAP B6

Sitting between Leblon and Barra beaches, Praia de São Conrado is one of Rio's top surfing beaches, with waves averaging 3–5 ft (1–1.5 m). The anvil-shaped peak, Pedra da Gávea, towering over the east end of the beach, is popular with rock climbers. The west end, known as Praia do Pepino, is a popular landing spot for hang-gliders taking off from Pedra Bonita. It is essential to check if the water is safe for bathing.

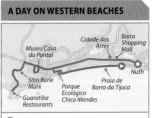

A DAY ON WESTERN BEACHES

▶ **MORNING**

Start the day with a bike ride on the cycle paths beside **Praia de Barra da Tijuca** (BikeRio is a city-wide bicycle rental service, see p105). Dotted along the seafront are snack stalls where you can stop for a chilled *agua de coco* (coconut water) drunk straight from the shell, and watch the surfers tackle huge rollers coming in off the Atlantic Ocean. Continue to **Parque Ecológico Chico Mendes** in Recreio dos Bandeirantes, for a walk around its mangroves, looking out for caiman and other protected wildlife. Return your bike, then go for lunch at one of the area's renowned open-air seafood restaurants (see p100) overlooking the marshes of **Guaratiba**.

AFTERNOON

In the afternoon, take a guided tour around the magnificent house and gardens of **Sítio Burle Marx**, and visit the wonderful **Museu Casa do Pontal** (see p97). In the evening, take your pick from one of the dozens of restaurants in the Barra shopping mall (see p101) for dinner, followed by a concert at the stunning **Cidade das Artes** (see p97). If you still have some energy left, round off the night with Rio's elite at one of its trendiest nightclubs, **Nuth** (see p53).

Cidade das Artes

See map on pp97–9

Places to Eat

1 Barraca do Pepê

MAP B6 ▪ Av do Pepê,
Quiosque 11, Barra da Tijuca
▪ (21) 2433 1400 ▪ $

A *Carioca* surfers' institution, this
beach-side snack bar was set up by
a surf star in the 1970s, and offers
great sandwiches and smoothies.

2 Benkei Asiático

MAP B5 ▪ Shopping
Metropolitano Barra, Av Abelardo
Bueno 1300, Barra da Tijuca ▪ (21)
3095 9132 ▪ $$$

Hungry shoppers can choose between
dishes from Japan to India, at this
branch of the popular chain led by
chef Marina Tasakhi.

3 Cozzi

MAP B5 ▪ Estrada de
Jacarepaguá 6508, Anil ▪ (21) 3442
2515 ▪ $$

It's worth tracking down this great
restaurant in its isolated – though
safe – neighborhood, for its delicious
Italian cuisine and welcoming,
relaxed atmosphere.

4 222 Contemporâneo

MAP B6 ▪ Hotel Royal Tulip, Av
Aquarela do Brasil 75, São Conrado
▪ (21) 3323 2200 ▪ $$$

With stunning beach-side views, this
smart restaurant offers modern
global cuisine with imaginative flair.

5 Oasis

MAP B6 ▪ Estrada do Joá 136,
São Conrado ▪ (21) 3322 3144 ▪ $$$

Lying at the foot of Pedra Bonita, this
well-established barbecue restaurant
also serves excellent Catupiry cheese
pastéis (pastries), a *Carioca* favorite.

6 Bira

MAP A6 ▪ Estrada da Vendinha,
68 A, Grumari ▪ (21) 2410 1434 ▪
Open noon–5pm Thu–Sun ▪ $$

Feast on fresh fish at one of Rio de
Janeiro's most romantic open-air
restaurants, with spectacular views
over the Restinga da Marambaia.

PRICE CATEGORIES

For a three-course meal for one with half
a bottle of wine, taxes and extra charges.
Prices are quoted in US dollars.

$ under $25 $$ $25–50 $$$ over $50

7 Taco & Chilli

MAP B6 ▪ Carrefour, Av das
Américas 5150, Barra da Tijuca
▪ (21) 3216 1550 ▪ $

This simple little restaurant serves
tasty tacos and other Mexican fare;
a well-priced option for the area.

Pobre Juan in Fashion Mall

8 Pobre Juan

MAP B6 ▪ Fashion Mall, Estrada
da Gávea 899, São Conrado ▪ (21)
3252 2637 ▪ $$$

This steakhouse has won awards for
both its fine cuisine and wine list.

9 Rio Brasa

MAP B6 ▪ Av Ayrton Senna
2541, Barra da Tijuca ▪ (21) 2199
9191 ▪ $$

This buffet-style *churrascaria* offers
a range of international dishes.

10 Zuka

MAP B6 ▪ Barra Shopping, Av
das Américas 4666, Barra da Tijuca
▪ (21) 2512 8545 ▪ $$$

Specializing in contemporary Italian
cuisine, Zuka has a cozy atmosphere,
despite its mega-mall setting.

Shopping Malls

1 Américas Shopping
MAP B6 ■ Av das Américas 15500 ■ (21) 2442 9902 ■ www.americasshopping.com.br ■ Open 10am–10pm Mon–Sat, 11am–9pm Sun

Recreio's mall has 240 stores, plus a 12-screen cinema and an ice-rink.

2 Barra Shopping
MAP B6 ■ Av das Américas 4666 ■ (21) 3089 1051 ■ www.barrashopping.com.br ■ Open 10am–10pm Mon–Sat, 1–9pm Sun

Brazil's biggest mall with more than 700 stores and many restaurants.

3 Barra World
MAP B6 ■ Alfredo Baltazar Silveira 580 ■ (21) 3388 6228 ■ barraworld.com ■ Open 10am–10pm Mon–Sat, 3–9pm Sun

This family-friendly shopping mall provides a variety of free entertainment during the week.

4 Downtown
MAP B6 ■ Av das Américas 500 ■ (21) 2494 7072 ■ downtown.com.br ■ Open 8am–10pm Mon–Sat, 1–9pm Sun

A city within the city, open-air streets are lined with shops, restaurants, and a cinema.

5 Fashion Mall
MAP B6 ■ Estrada da Gávea 899 ■ (21) 2111 4444 ■ www.fashionmall.com.br ■ Open 10am–10pm Mon–Sat, 3–9pm Sun

Specializing in high-end designer fashion, this luxurious mall has 120 stores representing top Brazilian and international brands, as well as gourmet restaurants, cinema, and theater.

6 Millennium
MAP B6 ■ Av das Américas 7707 ■ (21) 2438 8220 ■ www.shoppingmillennium.com ■ Open 10am–10pm Mon–Sat, noon–9pm Sun

Family-centric Millennium specializes in everything for the house and home, and also has a pet shop.

7 New York City Center
MAP B6 ■ Av das Américas 5000 ■ (21) 3089 1051 ■ www.barrashopping.com.br ■ Open 10am–10pm Mon–Sat, 1–9pm Sun

This mall has a wide range of stores, as well as restaurants, a cinema, and a four-storey sports center.

8 Rio Design Barra
MAP B6 ■ Av das Américas 7777 ■ (21) 2430 3024 ■ www.riodesignbarra.com.br ■ Open 10am–10pm Mon–Sat, 3–9pm Sun

Focusing on beauty and fashion, this mall has more than 160 stores.

9 Via Parque
MAP B6 ■ Av Ayrton Senna 3000 ■ (21) 2430 5100 ■ www.viaparqueshopping.com.br ■ Open 10am–10pm Mon–Sat, 1–9pm Sun

Offering the complete retail experience, including CitiBank Hall, one of Rio's largest concert venues.

10 Village Mall
MAP B6 ■ Av das Américas 3900 ■ (21) 3003 4177 ■ www.shoppingvillagemall.com.br ■ Open 11am–11pm Mon–Sat, 1–9pm Sun

One of Rio's newest malls, Village Mall is firmly upscale, with top fashion stores, fine-dining options, and the 1,060-seat Teatro Bradesco.

Village Mall, Barra da Tijuca

See map on pp96–7

Streetsmart

The colorful Escadaria Selarón, Lapa

Getting To and Around Rio de Janeiro

Arriving by Air

Rio de Janeiro is served by two airports: **Antônio Carlos Jobim**, for international flights; and **Santos Dumont**, for domestic flights.

Rio's international airport, which lies 9 miles (15 km) north of the city center, is often referred to by its former name – Galeão. It also handles some domestic flights. The airport has a Riotur information center, 24-hour ATMs, post office, shops, and a currency exchange. Taxis and shuttle buses connect to the city and the domestic airport, Santos Dumont. Taxis to Ipanema and Copacabana cost about US$25 from Galeão. Allow at least 1 hour to get there during rush hours.

The best airport buses are the **Real Auto** air-conditioned coaches, which leave from terminals 1 and 2 and connect to the city center bus station (**Rodoviária Novo Rio**), Aeroporto Santos Dumont, Glória, Flamengo, Botafogo, Copacabana, Ipanema, Gávea, São Conrado, and Barra da Tijuca. Departures are every 30 minutes between 5:30am and 11:30pm, costing approx. US$6.

Rio's domestic airport lies half a mile (1 km) south of the city center. It offers shuttle flights to São Paulo and onward connections to many of Brazil's other state capitals and major cities. Taxis to Ipanema and Copacabana are around US$15 from

here. Buy a ticket at the taxi booths inside the terminal. Shuttles from the international airport stop here en route to Copacabana and Ipanema.

Arriving by Bus

International and interstate buses leave from the downtown bus station Rodoviária Novo Rio. It has recently reopened after an extensive overhaul and has a Riotur information booth (for hotel bookings), left luggage, ATMs, money exchanges, shops, a post office, and cafés. Taxis to Ipanema and Copacabana cost around US$10. Be careful outside the bus station, however, as the area attracts thieves.

Getting Around by Bus

Rio city buses are plentiful and inexpensive, operating daily from early till late. Buses are clearly labeled with their destination on the front, though you'll need to flag the bus down at the stop. They should be avoided when getting to and from the airport with all your belongings, however, as well as at night, when petty theft is common. In 2011, an express bus service called BRS was introduced, serving Copacabana, Leblon, Ipanema, and downtown Rio. Exclusive bus lanes and streamlined bus stops have cut journey times dramatically. Further rapid transit lanes

are being built in time for the 2016 Olympic Games, connecting the districts of Santa Cruz and Barra da Tijuca, home of the Olympic Village, to the rest of the city.

By Metro

The best means of public transport in the city, Rio's metro system – **MetrôRio** – runs from the north to Ipanema through the city center. It is safe, clean, reliable, and cheap. There are two lines with 35 stations, as well as inter-connecting MetrôRio bus services going to Barra da Tijuca and Jacarepaguá. Line 4 is being constructed, adding six more stations between Ipanema and Barra da Tijuca, and scheduled to open by the 2016 Olympics. It's worth taking a taxi from outlying areas to the nearest metro station.

Tickets

Metro tickets for a single journey (*unitário*) are available; valid for 3 days from the date of purchase, with a R$1 refund if you return the ticket afterwards. Pre-paid tickets (*pre-pago*) can be purchased for multiple journeys with no date restrictions. Pre-paid tickets are also valid on the MetrôRio bus service, and the express buses.

By Sea

A cheap and efficient ferry service connects Rio to Niterói, and beyond to Ilha

Grande and Angra dos Reis. **CCR Barcas** ferries depart from downtown, Praça XV de Novembro, with regular daily departures from 5:40am to 11:30pm. The journey is 20 minutes to Niterói.

By Taxi

Taxis can be the most comfortable way of getting around Rio, and not necessarily the most expensive form of transport if, for instance, you share a ride to the airport. Standard (comum) licensed yellow-and-blue taxis are the most common; they use a 2-tariff meter system, indicated by a flag on the dashboard. Tariff 1 is all day up to 10pm; tariff 2 applies after 10pm, all day Sundays, and public holidays. While all licensed taxis operate from hotels or the taxi stands in each neighborhood,

not all of them you find on the streets are from cooperative service.

By Car

Driving in Rio is the least favored way of getting around the city. There are many confusing one-way systems, parking is difficult and unsafe, traffic jams can be horrendous, and Cariocas drive quickly and aggressively. Renting a car is costly, so it is worth organizing a deal before leaving for Brazil. Most major car rentals are represented in the city and have offices at the airports. It is wise to avoid driving after dark.

By Bicycle

With an increasing number of bicycle lanes alongside the beaches, and around the Lagoa Rodrigo de Freitas, cycling in Rio is

becoming a popular form of transport. There are bike hire companies in most beach-side neighborhoods, and the government-sponsored **Bike Rio** service has 600 orange-colored bicycles to rent at 60 Metrô stations.

On Foot

In many ways, Rio is the perfect city for walkers, with its miles of sandy beaches, wide expanse of shady parks and gardens, and most of all, a friendly outdoor city culture. During the day, the city center and beach neighborhoods of Ipanema, Leblon, and Copacabana can be explored on foot, while longer distances are best covered by taxi or metro. Use taxis at night for safety reasons. Rio's favelas should also be avoided alone on foot, by day or by night.

Practical Information

Passports and Visas

Brazil operates a reciprocal visa policy; as such, EU citizens do not require tourist visas to visit Brazil for up to 90 days (renewable for another 90 days). Visitors from other countries, including the USA, Canada, Australia, and New Zealand, do. Visas are mandatory for any visitor who plans to stay in the country for longer than 180 days or who plans to work in Brazil.

Customs Regulations and Immigration

On arrival in Brazil, visitors will be given an entry/exit card, one copy of which will be kept by immigration officials, and the other will be needed on departure.

Travel Insurance

Visitors to Brazil should arrange travel insurance in advance. Robberies and snatch thefts are not uncommon and crimes should be reported immediately at a police station (delegacia). When reporting a crime, make sure to request an official printed report (denuncia). Health insurance is necessary as ambulances take patients without insurance to public hospitals, where conditions may be poor.

Health

Visitors to Brazil can be asked to provide a yellow fever vaccination certificate upon entering the country. It is also a good idea to have vaccines for tetanus, polio, and hepatitis A. Dengue fever, which is transmitted by mosquitoes, is present in Rio, but there is no vaccine for this. Private health care, dental treatment, and pharmacies are of the same standards as in Europe and the USA.

There are a number of private medical centers that have English-speaking staff, including **Hospital Samaritano** and **Clínica Galdino Campos**.

Pharmacies, or farmácias, can be found throughout Rio, some of which are open 24 hours. Many prescription drugs, including antibiotics, are available over the counter. As in Europe and North America, cosmetics, insect repellents, and sun protection can be purchased at pharmacies. The morning-after pill (la pílula do dia seguinte) can also be obtained from pharmacies.

HIV, AIDS, and other STDs are widespread in Brazil, with the highest incidence in larger cities, including Rio. All types of contraceptives are widely available at pharmacies throughout the city. **Disque-AIDS** is a helpline for people with AIDS or for those seeking advice: call (21) 2518 2221, noon–6pm Mon–Fri.

Insect Bites

In urban Rio, dangerous insects and arachnids are few and far between. However, mosquitoes are found in the city, particularly during hot and wet periods, and they commonly carry and transmit dengue fever – a viral infection with severe flu-like symptoms. Visitors can protect themselves by using a good mosquito repellent (containing DEET), wearing long, light-colored clothing, and choosing accommodation that is air-conditioned.

Sunburn

The tropical sun is strong, even on overcast days. Use sunscreen of at least SPF 30. Children or those with sensitive skin should not use anything below SPF 50. Try to avoid direct sunlight between 11am and 1pm.

Personal Security

Rio's police are making dramatic efforts to improve the safety of the city, partly for the benefit of visitors to the 2016 Olympic Games. The risk of petty theft remains real, however, especially on buses. Credit cards and other valuables are best stored in a zipped money belt under your clothes or left in a safe at the hotel. Muggings are also common. It is best not to challenge the perpetrators. Avoid long walks after dark and use ATMs inside banks, malls, and supermarkets. Take licensed cabs from designated stands, hotels, or airport booths.

DEAT is Rio's English-speaking tourist police

unit, based in Leblon at the far end of Ipanema. At other police stations, generally only Portuguese is spoken.

Favelas should generally be avoided except on organized tours with groups who contribute part of their income to the community. During the day, the city center and beach neighborhoods of Ipanema, Leblon, and Copacabana can be explored on foot. Longer distances, particularly in spread-out western beach districts like Barra da Tijuca, are best covered by taxi or metro. The city center, beaches, and quiet streets should be avoided after dark, as should Parque do Flamengo.

Take care around the Rodoviária Novo Rio, where thieves operate. Prostitution is rife along Copacabana's Avenida Atlântica and in the various clubs and cafés that run along its length. Many prostitutes double up as muggers and are famous for plying patrons, both male and female, with "Boa Noite Cinderelas," or "Good Night Cinderellas" – drinks that have been drugged. Victims can wake up in an hotel room empty of all their belongings.

Women Travelers

Rio is a very welcoming city and women are treated courteously. To ward off unsolicited advances, firmly say *me deixa em paz, por favor* (leave me alone, please).

Gay and Lesbian Travelers

Rio is one of the most open-minded cities in Brazil; gays and lesbians have long been a part of the community, though homophobic jokes and macho attitudes are still common. Copacabana and Ipanema are the most liberal areas, and where there are many gay-friendly bars and nightclubs, particularly along Rua Farme de Amoedo in Ipanema and the stretch of beach opposite *(see p32)*.

DIRECTORY

CONSULATES

Argentina
📞 (21) 2553 1646
🌐 crioj.cancilleria.gov.ar

Australia
📞 (21) 3824 4624
🌐 dfat.gov.au/missions/countries/brri.html

Canada
📞 (21) 2543 3004
🌐 canadainternational.gc.ca/brazil-bresil/

UK
📞 (21) 2555 9600
🌐 reinounido.org.br

USA
📞 (21) 3823 2000
🌐 riodejaneiro.usconsulate.gov

EMERGENCY SERVICES

Ambulance (Ambulância)
📞 192

DEAT
MAP L5 ■ Av Afrânio de Melo Franco 159
📞 (21)2332 2924/2885/2889

Fire Department (Bombeiros)
📞 193

Police (Polícia)
📞 190

HEALTH

Disque-AIDS
Open noon–8pm Mon–Fri
📞 (21) 2518 2221

HOSPITALS/WALK-IN CLINICS

MAP R3 ■ Clínica Galdino Campos
Av NS. de Copacabana 492, Copacabana
📞 (21) 2548 9966
🌐 galdinocampos.com.br

Hospital Samaritano
MAP G4 ■ Rua Bambina 98, Botafogo
📞 (21) 2537 9722/2535 4000
🌐 hsamaritano.com.br

PHARMACIES

Drogaria Cristal
MAP H3 ■ Rua Marquês de Abrantes 27, Flamengo
📞 (21) 2225 7319

Drogaria Pacheco
MAP Q4 ■ Av N. Sra. de Copacabana 534, Copacabana
📞 (21) 3208 4600

Farma Life
MAP B6 ■ Av das Américas 3501, Barra da Tijuca
📞 (21) 2239 1178

Drogarias Wilson
MAP L5 ■ Rua Dias Ferreira 618, Leblon
📞 (21) 2511 7000

LOST PROPERTY OFFICES

International airport
Terminal One
📞 (21) 3398 4152/3044
Terminal Two
📞 (21) 3398 2013

MetrôRio
customer service desk at Carioca station
📞 (21) 4003 2111
📞 0800 595 1111

Rodoviária Novo Rio
📞 (21) 3213 1820

Beaches

There are strong currents and rip tides at many of Rio's beaches and the water is chilly. Numbered lifeguard stations (postos) are dotted along Copacabana and Ipanema beaches, open daily from 8am to 8pm with flags indicating unsafe areas for swimming. Beaches within Guanabara Bay, particularly Flamengo and Botafogo, are heavily polluted, so swimming here is not advised. Stick to the beaches further out in the Atlantic Ocean, at Copacabana and beyond.

During the day, Rio's bigger beaches are generally well policed, but it's better to bring as little as possible with you and stay alert. Personal items left unattended are likely to be stolen, especially when it gets crowded.

Rio de Janeiro may appear liberal, but it is actually quite conservative, particularly as regards public behavior. Going topless on the beach is regarded as extremely vulgar and could lead to arrest. Wearing Brazilian "dental floss" (filo dental) bikinis, however, which leave little to the imagination, is quite acceptable.

Currency and Banking

The Brazilian currency, the real (R$, pronounced Hey-owl; plural reais – pronounced Hey-ice), is divided into 100 centavos. The largest note is R$100; coins are 5, 10, 25, 50 centavos, and R$1. Small shops struggle to change R$100, R$50,

and R$20 notes, making R$10 and R$5 the most commonly used notes.

Automatic Teller Machines (ATMs), or caixas electronicas, found throughout Rio, are the easiest way to get cash. Withdrawals are limited to between R$600 and R$1,000 per transaction and two transactions per day; though some banks may reduce the limit to R$300 per day. For safety reasons, ATMs stop cash withdrawals after 10pm, or earlier, until 6am. Always try to use them during the day.

American Express, Visa, MasterCard, Diners Club, and other major international credit cards are accepted at most places, including ATMs, throughout Rio.

Euros and US dollars are the most widely accepted foreign currencies for exchange in Rio, and US dollars are also accepted by large hotels.

Major banks change foreign currency, but the exchange rates are usually poorer than those at casas de câmbio (exchange offices). Ask for notes in a range of denominations. Be sure to keep a few smaller notes in your pockets and the rest stashed away safely under your clothing in a money belt.

Travelers' checks are next to useless in Brazil, where surcharges and taxes for their usage are prohibitively high in the few banks that accept them. It is more convenient to use a credit card while making major expenses, such as hotel bills.

Internet and Telephone

The cheapest and easiest way to keep in touch is via social network sites and online phone apps, such as Skype. There are plenty of Internet cafés in Rio, especially in Botafogo, Copacabana, Ipanema, and Leblon. Most hotels have Wi-Fi, and some even offer wireless broadband in rooms.

You can use your own cell phone in Brazil, as most international networks have roaming contracts with Brazil, using the GSM network. However, dialing charges can be high and users pay extraordinarily expensive rates when receiving calls from outside Rio state. Alternatively, you can buy a SIM card on arrival. Competition between the main Brazilian phone companies is fierce, with sometimes bewildering offers to try to tempt you to sign up; the pay-as-you-go (pre-pago) deal is probably the simplest option.

Public telephones, known as orelhões (big ears) because of their unusual shape, are increasingly becoming rare in Rio. They accept cartões telefônicos (phone cards), available at newsstands and post offices, but not coins. For long-distance calls, dial the three- or four-digit code of a prestadora (service provider) before the area or country code. You can use any provider; the most common are **Vivo** (15), **Claro/NET** (21), and **Oi** (31).

TV and Newspapers

Brazil's TV Globo is one of the largest television producers in the world and is famous for its soaps. Most hotels in Rio only show Brazilian television. Some of the bigger hotels offer satellite TV, which has European channels, CNN, Al-Jazeera, and BBC World News.

The principal papers and news magazines are *O Globo*, *A Folha de São Paulo*, *Veja*, *Istoé*, and *Epoca*. *Veja*, which comes out on Fridays, has a useful arts section with listings for shows, concerts, and other events. *The Rio Times*, a free monthly English newspaper, is distributed to hotels, restaurants, and other outlets.

Postal Services

Correios (post offices) are widespread and can be identified by a yellow and blue sign. Postcards are cheap but the system of pricing for letters and parcels sent to Europe or the USA is complex and prices can vary greatly from office to office and clerk to clerk. Express deliveries are known as SEDEX; service, however, is notoriously slow and packages have been known to disappear. For valuable items, international couriers, such as Fedex and DHL, are more reliable.

Most post offices operate from 9am to 5pm Monday to Friday, from 10am to 1pm on Saturdays, and are closed on Sundays. A few open for longer at weekends.

Opening Hours

Banks are open on weekdays from 9 or 10am until 3 or 4pm, but currency exchanges often stay open an hour later. Post office timings vary but they are usually open from 9am to 5pm. Shops are open from 9am until 6pm from Monday to Saturday, and malls stay open in the week from 10am until 10 or 11pm, later on Saturdays, and some on Sunday afternoons too.

Time Difference

Rio is on Brazilian Standard Time, three hours behind GMT and three hours ahead of Eastern Standard Time for most of the year. Clocks go forward one hour on the third Sunday in October, after which Rio is two hours behind GMT and two hours ahead of Eastern Standard Time, until the third Sunday in February, when they go back one hour again.

Electrical Appliances

There is no standard voltage in Brazil. Electricity comes in both 200 volts and 127 volts AC. Two-pronged plugs are used, either round or flat pin. However, most houses and even hotel rooms have both.

Driving License

A full driving license is required to drive in Brazil; most car rental companies also require drivers to be at least 25 years of age.

Weather and What to Wear

Rio is beautiful at any time of the year. It is wet and warm from November to February, and dry and sunny during the rest of the year. The most popular times to visit are December and during Carnaval, which usually falls in February or March.

Bring clothing for temperatures that can range from 95°F (35°C) to 59°F (15°C). Rio is an informal city and gives you the opportunity to dress down; men rarely wear a suit and tie. Flip-flops (*chinelos* or *havaianas*) or sandals are commonly worn in the beach neighborhoods, while light walking shoes are good for the city center and for forest walks. Leave expensive watches, smartphones, and jewelry at home.

Visitor Information

Riotur, the city's official tourist authority, has information booths all over Rio. It produces the free bi-monthly *Rio Guide*, with information and events listings in both Portuguese and English.

Disabled Travelers

While facilities for visitors with disabilities are generally poor in Brazil, Rio is improving accessibility in airports, bus stations, malls, and some of the bigger hotels. Metro trains and stations have facilities, such as lifts and ramps, but the over-crowded buses make little allowance for wheelchair users. Especial Coop taxis have specially adapted cars and English-speaking drivers: (www.especialcooptaxirj.com.br; (021) 3295 9606). The Society for Accessible Travel and Hospitality (SATH) offers tips on its website (www.sath.org).

Trips and Tours

A wide range of tours around Rio is available from rock-climbing and helicopter rides to visits to the *favelas*. Tours of Rio's notorious shanty towns should only be undertaken with an authorized guide who contributes to the community. Guided walks are a great way for first-time visitors to get a taste of the city and to meet locals. Day trips farther afield, along the coast or inland, are also offered by tour companies.

Dining Tips

Cariocas tend to eat a light breakfast between 7 and 9am. Lunch, which is the main meal of the day, is usually between noon and 2pm. Dinner tends to be light, except on special occasions, and is mostly eaten after 9pm. At weekend lunchtimes, many restaurants serve the Brazilian national dish, *feijoada* – a thick meaty bean stew eaten with lime, manioc flour, rice, and greens, washed down with a shot of Brazilian raw cane rum, *cachaça*, and followed by a long siesta.

Portions in many restaurants can be huge; it is quite acceptable to ask the waiter to bring an extra plate and share a dish between two. Some upscale restaurants place bread, olives, cold meats, and cheeses, known as *petiscos*, on the table. These appetizers are not free, but form part of a cover (*couvert*), charged per person. To avoid paying, ask the waiter to take them away. Most restaurants will include a 10 percent service charge on the bill; otherwise, 10 percent is considered a normal tip.

Rio was some of the best *churrascarias* (Brazilian-style grilled meat restaurants) in the country, offering an all-you-can-eat feast for a fixed price.

Por-Kilo buffet restaurants are among the best-value eating options in Rio and are especially popular at lunchtimes. Diners choose from a selection of self-serve options, which are then weighed and priced at the counter.

The *prato feito*, or *prato de dia*, is an inexpensive set lunch offered by many side-street restaurants that comprises a starter, main course, dessert or juice, and coffee.

Vegetarians have a hard time in Brazil, though there are a few good options in Rio.

Brazil has a delicious and huge variety of fruits, from familiar mangoes and papayas to the uniquely Brazilian (*see p41*). Juice bars serve up wonderful mixes of these fruits, or you can buy them more cheaply in street markets.

Where to Stay

The vast majority of hotels are in Copacabana, Ipanema, and Leblon;

accommodation is more expensive, but much of the best dining, nightlife, and shopping is here, plus it is generally safer.

Many of the familiar international chains populate the beach-front districts. Smaller, more characterful boutique hotels and B&Bs can also be found, particularly in Santa Teresa and Gávea.

There are many hostels offering cheaper accommodation in shared dorms and private rooms. Most are in the beach neighborhoods – notably Botafogo, Copacabana, and Ipanema. There is also a growing number in Santa Teresa.

Staying at a *Carioca*'s home is one of the best ways of getting to know the city. **Cama e Café** offers home-stays all over the city, including homes of local artists in Santa Teresa. **Angatu** and **The Brazilian Beach House Company** offer luxurious private houses for rent.

Furnished apartments from agencies, such as **Flats in Rio**, are a great money-saving option; most can be rented for a week or more. The best have kitchens, washing machines, and TVs, as well as concierge services and daily room cleaning.

For visitors traveling with children, extra beds, cots, and babysitting services are almost always available in Brazilian hotels.

Reservations and Rates

High season is during Christmas and New Year as well as the two weeks around Carnaval when it is essential to book well in advance.

Discount rates are often available through booking websites, including **booking.com**, **hotels.com**, **Couchsurfing**, and **Airbnb**. These discounts can be up to 50 percent of the standard rate, especially if you reserve your room more than a few weeks in advance. Booking direct through the hotel's own website, however, often gives better rates than those found on the international websites.

DIRECTORY

RIOTUR INFORMATION BOOTHS

Aeroporto Internacional Antônio Carlos Jobim
((21) 3398 4077
((21) 3367 6213
Open daily

Barra da Tijuca
MAP B6 ■ Av do Pepê
Open 8am–6pm daily

Centro
MAP X2 ■ Rua Candelária 6
Open 9am–6pm Mon–Fri, 9am–3pm Sat

Copacabana
MAP R4 ■ Av Atlântica
((21) 2541 7522
Open 8am–8pm daily

Ipanema
MAP N5 ■ Rua Visconde de Pirajá
Open 8am–8pm daily

Lapa
MAP W4 ■ Av Mém de Sá
Open 10am–10pm daily

Shopping da Gávea
MAP K4 ■ Rua Marquês de São Vicente 52
Open 10am–10pm Mon–Sat, noon–9pm Sun

SOURCES OF INFORMATION

Alô Rio Tourism Hotline
((21) 2542 8080/8004

Turisrio Tourist Board
w turisrio.rj.gov.br

Rio Carnaval
w rio-carnival.net

Rio Gay Guide
w riogayguide.com

TOURS

Adventure activities
w rioxtreme.com

Birding & Wildlife Tours
w regua.co.uk

Cycling
w bikeinriotours.com

Diving
w pldivers.com.br

Driving Tours
w privatetours.com.br

Favela Tours
w favelatour.com.br
w favelatour.org

Guanabara Bay
w saveiros.com.br

Guided Walks
w culturalrio.com.br

Helicopter Tours
w helisight.com.br

Hang-Gliding
w justflyinrio.blogspot.com

Hiking
w riohiking.com.br

Rock Climbing
w climbinrio.com

ACCOMMODATIONS

Angatu
w angatu.com

Airbnb
w airbnb.com

Brazilian Beach House Company
w brazilianbeachhouse.com

Cama e Café
w camaecafe.com.br

Couchsurfing
w couchsurfing.com

Flats in Rio
w flatsinrio.com

Places to Stay

PRICE CATEGORIES
For a standard, double room per night (with breakfast if included), taxes, and extra charges.

$ under US$85 $$ US$85–200 $$$ over US$200

Luxury Hotels

Hotel Flórida
MAP H3 ▪ Rua Ferreira Viana 81, Catete ▪ (21) 2195 6800 ▪ $$
This refurbished hotel has more than 400 well-appointed rooms and a master suite each floor. It enjoys a central location if you are heading towards Lapa or downtown. The rooftop terrace offers impressive views of Flamengo Beach and Sugar Loaf Mountain.

Caesar Park
MAP N6 ▪ Av Vieira Souto 460, Ipanema ▪ (21) 2525 2525 ▪ www.sofitel.com ▪ $$$
Service is superb in Caesar Park, a business hotel overlooking Ipanema Beach. Views are excellent, as with the majority of Rio's tower-block hotels. There is 24-hour room service and beach facilities include sun-loungers, towels, and showers.

Copacabana Palace
MAP R3 ▪ Av Atlântica 1702, Copacabana ▪ (21) 2548 7070 ▪ www.copacabanapalace.com.br ▪ $$$
Copacabana's most famous and plush hotel features ocean-view suites that have housed princes, presidents, and visiting film stars. Portraits of many of the famous guests can be seen in the gallery. The older portion of the hotel has the best rooms.

Fasano
MAP P6 ▪ Av Vieira Souto 80, Ipanema ▪ (21) 3202 4000 ▪ www.fasano.com.br ▪ $$$
A world-class luxury hotel in Ipanema designed by Philippe Starck with a 1950s "Bossa Nova" look. The rooms are beautifully appointed with marble bathrooms and most have private balconies with sea views. The restaurant here is excellent, as is the rooftop infinity pool and salon spa on the first floor.

Ipanema Plaza
MAP N6 ▪ Rua Farme de Amoedo 34, Ipanema ▪ (21) 3687 2000 ▪ www.ipanemaplaza.com ▪ $$$
This hotel occupies a tall tower only a block from the sea at Ipanema's Arpoador end. The rooms on the "Ipanema floor" have clean modern lines and colors, along with Italian furniture. The top floor has a pool and offers great views of the Atlantic.

Marina Palace
MAP L6 ▪ Av Delfim Moreira 630, Leblon ▪ (21) 2529 5700 ▪ www.hotelmarina.com.br ▪ $$$
One of the better tower hotels, the Marina Palace is within walking distance of Leblon's restaurants and has 109 spacious rooms, free Wi-Fi, a pool, and a sauna. The upper floors offer great views of the ocean.

Pestana Rio Atlântica
MAP Q4 ▪ Av Atlântica 2964, Copacabana ▪ (21) 2548 6332 ▪ www.pestana.com ▪ $$$
The views out over Copacabana from this hotel's rooftop pool are some of the best in Rio. The rooms all have private balconies.

Radisson Barra
MAP B6 ▪ Av Lúcio Costa 3150, Barra da Tijuca ▪ (21) 3139 8000 ▪ www.atlanticahotels.com.br ▪ $$$
These twin towers right on the beach are the best choice for stays in the neighborhoods of Barra da Tijuca and Recreio dos Bandeirantes. The rooms are spacious and have balconies with sea views.

Royal Tulip São Conrado Beach
MAP B6 ▪ Rua Aquarela do Brasil 75, São Conrado ▪ (21) 3323 2200 ▪ www.royaltulipriodejaneiro.com ▪ $$$
This former grand 1970s hotel situated between Leblon and São Conrado recently underwent a major refurbishment and now has an on-site burger shop. The adjacent beach is secluded and the views are stunning.

Sofitel
MAP Q5 ▪ Av Atlântica 4240, Copacabana ▪ (21) 2525 1232 ▪ www.sofitel.com ▪ $$$
The fabulous views, excellent French rest-

aurant Le Pré Catalan (see p95), and quality service are matched by the luxurious rooms.

Sol Ipanema

MAP M6 ■ Av Viera Souto 320, Ipanema ■ (21) 2525 2020 ■ www. solipanema.com.br ■ $$$

This beachside four-star hotel is the Ipanema representative of the Best Western chain. Rooms are a little small with standard hotel furnishings. The higher floors are quieter. Facilities include fitness center and beauty parlor.

Windsor Barra

MAP B6 ■ Avenida Lucio Costa 2630, Barra da Tijuca ■ (21) 2195 5000 ■ www.windsorhoteis. com.br ■ $$$

This modern, business-oriented five-star hotel overlooks Barra da Tijuca beach; with spacious bedrooms, adjoining conference center, and rooftop pool with great views. Extra charge for Wi-Fi access.

Boutique and Designer Hotels

Casa Áurea

MAP V6 ■ Rua Áurea 80, Santa Teresa ■ (21) 2242 5830 ■ www.casaaurea. com.br ■ $

This informal, family-run budget boutique hostel sits in its own little garden patio on a Santa Teresa backstreet. Each room comes in a different shape, size, and color, and is decorated with art. The crowd is young and the staff speak a variety of languages, including English.

Casa Mango Mango

MAP V6 ■ Rua Joaquim Murtinho 587, Santa Teresa ■ (21) 2508 6440 ■ www.casa-mango mango.com ■ $

Santa Teresa's most arty boutique hotel lies next to the convent that gave the neighborhood its name. The public areas and ten rooms are decorated with works by local artists; there is also a separate chalet, with self-catering facilities, sleeping up to four people. The rooms offer wonderful views over the tropical gardens to the city center.

Corcovado Rio Hostel

MAP Q3 ■ Rua Conselheiro Lampreia 169, Cosme Velho ■ (21) 3228 3525 ■ www.casa32. com.br ■ $$

This hostel offers good-value private or shared rooms. The leafy surroundings and pool make for a country house atmosphere. They also arrange transfers to the airport or the beaches.

Rio Design

MAP Q5 ■ Rua Francisco Sá 17, Copacabana ■ (21) 3222 8800 ■ www. riodesignhotel.com ■ $$

Copacabana's only boutique hotel has a series of designer suites in a business-like, tall, narrow tower. The decor is minimalist, the furnishings are functional, and the service attentive.

Casa Mosquito

MAP G6 ■ 222, Rua Saint Roman, Copacabana ■ (21) 3586 5042 ■ www. casamosquito.com ■ $$$

Located up a steep winding street overlooking Copacabana and Ipanema, this beautiful boutique hotel has nine stylish suites featuring retro decor of the 1950s, including four that are inspired by famous Cariocas. A spa and outdoor pool add to its luxurious touches.

Hotel Santa Teresa

MAP V6 ■ Rua Almirante Alexandrino 660, Santa Teresa ■ (21) 3380 0200 ■ www.santa-teresa-hotel.com ■ $$$

The most exclusive boutique hotel in Santa Teresa; luxurious suites with hardwood flooring and designer furniture, plus spa and tropical gardens; its Tereze French restaurant is one of the finest in Rio.

La Maison

MAP D6 ■ Rua Sérgio Porto 58, Gávea ■ (21) 3205 3585 ■ www. lamaisonario.com ■ $$$

This sister boutique to La Suite is more under-stated and is a cab ride from the nearest beach, Leblon. It boasts fantastic views out to Corcovado. There are five rooms in assorted colors from hot pink to cool chinoiserie, designed on global themes.

Mama Ruisa

MAP V6 ■ Rua Santa Cristina 132, Santa Teresa ■ (21) 2508 8142 ■ www.mamaruisa.com ■ $$$

A charming, understated boutique hotel housed in a converted 18th-century mansion house in Santa Teresa. Each room is named after a different French cultural icon.

Marina All Suites
MAP L6 ▪ Av Delfim Moreira 696, Leblon ▪ (21) 3957 9375 ▪ www. marinaallsuites.com.br ▪ $$$
This plush sea-front hotel, which has hosted many celebrities, features 17 signature suites created by leading designers. It also offers 22 additional suites with lounges and home heaters, and has a great bar and restaurant.

Le Relais de Marambaia
MAP A6 ▪ Estrada Roberto Burle Marx 9346, Barra de Guaratiba ▪ (21) 2394 2544 ▪ www.lerelaisde marambaia.com.br ▪ $$$
A rarity among the high-rise complexes typical of Barra, this luxurious French-run boutique hotel ticks all the boxes for a hideaway haven. It has seven rooms, each with balcony; restaurant, pool and spa, and a terrace overlooking the ocean.

La Suite
MAP B6 ▪ Rua Jackson de Figueiredo 501, Joá ▪ (21) 3259 6123 ▪ www. lasuiterio.com ▪ $$$
Rio's finest boutique hotel overlooks the exclusive Joatinga beach. Each of its seven rooms and suites is painted a different color and has a lush marble bathroom to match. The overall theme blends modern and classical styles.

Mid-Priced Hotels

Debret
MAP Q4 ▪ Av Atlântica 3564, Copacabana ▪ (21) 3883 2034 ▪ www.debret. com ▪ $
Named for the French artist who painted some

of the first landscapes of Rio, this modest beach-front hotel has bright, airy rooms. Some suites have living areas with sofas, armchairs, and sturdy hardwood dining tables.

Regina
MAP H3 ▪ Rua Ferreira Viana 29, Flamengo ▪ (21) 3289 9999 ▪ www. hotelregina.com.br ▪ $
This solid, old hotel on one of Flamengo's quieter side streets has small but clean modern rooms, with free Wi-Fi. The buffet breakfasts are good and it's handy for downtown and the beaches.

Casa Cool Beans
MAP U6 ▪ Rua Laurinda Santos Lobo 146, Santa Teresa ▪ (21) 2262 0552 ▪ www.casacoolbeans. com ▪ $
This delightful B&B, spread over four floors, offers ten luxurious, tastefully decorated rooms, plus gardens, a pool, and a sundeck. All rooms have en-suite bathrooms and come with air conditioning, a mini bar, and complimentary Wi-Fi access. A Brazilian-style breakfast is also included.

Copacabana Mar
MAP R3 ▪ Rua Min. Viveiros de Castro 155, Copacabana ▪ (21) 3501 7900 ▪ www. copacabanamarhotel. com ▪ $$
This beach-front tower has comfortable rooms with minimalist, neutral decor and king-size beds. The hotel's business facilities are modern with free access to wireless Internet in all rooms.

Hotel Vermont
MAP N5 ▪ Rua Visconde de Pirajá 254, Ipanema ▪ (21) 3202 5500 ▪ www. hotelvermont.com.br ▪ $$
The better rooms in this hotel are on the higher floors and have decent views, while the rooms on the lower floors overlook a concrete wall. This is one of the mid-priced options in the city and is popular with the gay community.

Ipanema Inn
MAP N6 ▪ Rua Maria Quiteria 27, Ipanema ▪ (21) 2523 6092 ▪ www. ipanemainn.com.br ▪ $$
There are good beach views from the upper floors of this tower, which is tucked behind the Caesar Park hotel in Ipanema. The hotel has plain but well-maintained rooms, and is close to the beach and popular shopping streets.

Mar Ipanema
MAP M5 ▪ Rua Visconde de Pirajá 539, Ipanema ▪ (21) 3875 9191 ▪ www. maripanema.com ▪ $$
This tower lies in the heart of Ipanema, near the beach and shopping areas. The simply decorated rooms have wooden floors and black and white prints of Rio. Use of beach chairs and towels is free.

Savoy Othon Travel
MAP Q4 ▪ Av Nossa Senhora de Copacabana 995 ▪ (21) 2125 0200 ▪ www.othon.com.br ▪ $$
The Savoy is part of the prosperous Brazilian Othon chain, but its rates are lower than many similar hotels in the area. Rooms on the upper floors boast fantastic views of Copacabana.

Quinta Azul

MAP V6 ■ Rua Almirante Alexandrino 256, Santa Teresa ■ (21) 3253 1021 ■ $$$

Housed in a blue-painted colonial building, this centrally located boutique *pousada* offers chic, modern rooms decorated with antique furniture. Some rooms have balconies overlooking the hills of the neighborhood.

Apartments and Houses

Cama e Café

MAP U6 ■ Rua Progresso 67, Santa Teresa ■ (21) 2225 4366 ■ www. camaecafe.com.br ■ $

This homestay company has over 100 houses on their books, mostly in Santa Teresa but also all around Rio; from simple rooms in student houses to suites in Rio's most luxurious mansions. Guests can enjoy as much privacy or as much of the company of their host as they choose.

Copacabana Holiday

MAP R3 ■ Rua Barata Ribeiro 90A, Copacabana ■ (21) 2542 1525 ■ www.copacabana holiday.com.br ■ $

These rental apartments are found in Copacabana, Ipanema, and Leblon, and many of them are located along the beach front. Some of the locations are very good value.

Copacabana One Flat

MAP P4 ■ Rua Pompeu Loureiro 99, Copacabana ■ (21) 2255 3908 ■ $

These simple, small apartments come with a concierge service and sit six blocks from Ipanema and Copacabana beaches, near to Lagoa Rodrigo de Freitas.

Fantastic Rio

(21) 3507 7491 ■ fantasticrio.br.tripod. com ■ $–$$$

These studios and apartments, with up to five bedrooms as well as one- or two-floor penthouses, can be found throughout the city. It is one of the most established rental companies in Rio.

Angatu

www.angatu.com ■ $$

This company provides luxury private homes as well as private islands with cabins and yachts in the Paraty, Angra dos Reis, and Ilha Grande area. The service is excellent with full transfers available.

The Brazilian Beach House Company

(+598) 2600 9542 ■ www. brazilianbeachhouse.com ■ $$

This British-run company offers luxurious beach and town houses throughout Rio de Janeiro, as well as some beautiful properties in Búzios, Paraty, and elsewhere around Brazil.

Mercure Barra da Tijuca

MAP B6 ■ Av do Pepê 56, Barra da Tijuca ■ (21) 2153 1200 ■ www. mercure.com ■ $$

Set on Praia do Pepê, this large modern complex has 135 apartments with full hotel facilities, including pool, restaurant, sauna, and gym.

Mercure Rio de Janeiro Arpoador

MAP P6 ■ Rua Francisco Otaviano 61, Ipanema ■ (21) 2113 8600 ■ www. mercure.com ■ $$

The apartments in this tower overlook Ipanema Beach. The facilities are similar to a hotel – there is room service, Wi-Fi, gym, pool, and a sauna.

Rio Apartments

MAP N5 ■ Rua Rainha Elizabeth 85, Copacabana ■ (21) 2247 6221 ■ www. rioapartments.se ■ $$

This company has apartments in Copacabana, Ipanema, and Leblon, that range from budget to comfortable. Many of the latter have leisure facilities, concierge, room service, and chauffeur-driven car hire.

Transamerica Prime Barra

MAP B6 ■ Avenida Gastão Senges 395, Barra da Tijuca ■ (21) 2123 7000 ■ www.transamerica group.com.br ■ $$

Spacious apartments, only a short walk from the beach and Barra's shops and nightlife, with Wi-Fi, pools, a restaurant, and room service. Great views of Pedra da Gávea.

Budget Hotels and Hostels

Atlantis Copacabana

MAP P5 ■ Rua Bulhões de Carvalho 61, Copacabana ■ (21) 2521 1142 ■ www.atlantis hotel.com.br ■ $

Small and simple air-conditioned rooms, and a two-minute walk from Copacabana and Ipanema beaches. Big breakfasts and a rooftop pool.

For a key to hotel price categories see p112

Casa 16

MAP M5 ▪ Rua Barão da Torre 175, Casa 16, Ipanema ▪ (21) 2247 1384 ▪ www.casa16 ipanema.com ▪ $

This French-owned hostel has two single rooms and one private room that can accommodate up to four guests. The hostel is quiet, but it is near many good restaurants and bars, and three blocks from the beach.

Che Lagarto Hostel

MAP M5 ▪ Rua Paul Redfern 48, Ipanema ▪ (21) 2512 8076 ▪ www. chelagarto.com ▪ $

This Argentinian, alligator-themed hostel chain is a popular party venue. Unlike most hostels, they do not offer a shuttle service. Another branch in Copacabana.

Ipanema Beach House

MAP M5 ▪ Rua Barão da Torre 485, Ipanema ▪ (21) 3202 2693 ▪ www. ipanemahouse.com ▪ $

This is one of Rio's more upmarket hostels. Rooms and dorms are gathered around a pool and garden bar area with a kitchen and free Wi-Fi. The central location is enviable and Ipanema Beach is a short walk away.

Lemon Spirit Hostel

MAP L5 ▪ Rua Cupertino Durão 56, Leblon ▪ (21) 2294 1853 ▪ www. lemonspirit.com ▪ $

This small hostel, which has a tiny back patio and a little bar, is one of the very few cheap options in Leblon. It occupies a converted town house with four- and six-bed dormitories.

Maze Inn

MAP H3 ▪ 414, Rua Tavares Bastos, Catete ▪ (21) 2558 5547 ▪www.jazzrio.com ▪ $

This arty hostel is in one of Rio's safest *favelas*, Tavares Bastos, with private rooms or dorm beds. Brit expat owner Bob Nadkarni is famously welcoming, and on the first Friday of the month there is live jazz and *bossa nova* on its terrace that overlooks Guanabara Bay.

Oztel

MAP P5 ▪ Rua Pinheiro Guimaraes 91 ▪ (21) 3042 1853 ▪ www.oztel. com.br ▪ $

Located at the Lagoa end of Botafogo, this trendy hostel is one of Rio's best. Otzel borders on being a hotel and it helped to raise the standards for hostels across Rio. Offers suites as well as dorms. Lounge, TV room, and popular bar. Good for public transport.

Rio Hostel Santa Teresa

MAP V5 ▪ Rua Joaquim Murtinho 351, Santa Teresa ▪ (21) 3852 0827 ▪ www.riohostel.com ▪ $

This hostel is built on the side of one of Santa Teresa's steep hills. It has its own pool and many of the rooms offer wonderful views of the city. Rio Hostel has another branch close to Ipanema and Copacabana beaches.

Sun Rio Hostel

MAP H4 ▪ Praia de Botafogo 462, Casa 5, Botafogo ▪ (21) 2226 0461 ▪ www.sunrio hostel.com.br ▪ $

The best small hostel in Botafogo, Sun Rio is situated in a converted town house close to Botafogo's excellent restaurants and shops. Rooms and dorms are scrupulously clean. Some rooms have private bathrooms and air-conditioning. Free Wi-Fi.

Terra Brasilis Hostel

MAP V5 ▪ Rua Murtinho Nobre 156, Santa Teresa ▪ (21) 3439 0037 ▪ www. brasilishostel.com ▪ $

This converted old mansion offers private rooms or dorm beds; it's spick and span, with a warm laid-back vibe. Breakfast is served on the patio, Wi-Fi access is free, and the views from the balconies are stunning.

Z.Bra Hostel

MAP E6 ▪ Av Gral San Martin 1212, Leblon ▪ (21) 3596 2386 ▪ www. zbrahostel.com ▪ $

This hip and colorful hostel has some tiny private rooms and cheaper dorms that sleep up to nine. Only a block from the beach and with helpful staff, it offers great value for money for the area. Beach gear can be rented for free.

SESC Copacabana

MAP Q4 ▪ Rua Domingos Ferreira 160, Copacabana ▪ (21) 2548 1088 ▪ www.sescrio.org. br ▪ $$

This cultural center, built in a style made famous by the Brazilian architect Oscar Niemeyer (see p72), features a theater, cinema, and hotel just one block from the beach. The atmosphere is quiet and the rooms are clean, modern, and very well maintained.

Hotels in Rio State

Bromelias Pousada and Spa

MAP A2 ▪ **Rodovia Rio-Santos (BR–101) Km 558, Graúna, Paraty** ▪ **(21) 3371 2791** ▪ **www.pousadabromelias.com.br** ▪ **$$**
Featuring luxury *cabanas* set in the heart of the Mata Atlântica rain forest, this hotel spa offers a range of relaxing treatments, from *reiki* to aromatherapy massage. The hotel has a pool, tennis courts, and a decent restaurant.

Hotel Chalés Terra Nova

MAP A2 ▪ **Estrada do Parque Nacional Km 4.5, Parque Nacional do Itatiaia** ▪ **(024) 3352 1458** ▪ **www.chalesterranova.com.br** ▪ **$$**
With charming *cabanas* on the edge of the lush green rain forest, this hotel features a pool in a peacock- and hummingbird-filled tropical garden. The hotel also organizes a number of light adventure activities for guests.

Pousada da Alcobaça

MAP B2 ▪ **Rua Agostino Goulão 298, Correas, Petrópolis** ▪ **(024) 2221 1240** ▪ **www.pousadada alcobaca.com.br** ▪ **$$**
This enchanting *pousada* near Petrópolis offers 11 tastefully furnished rooms in an early 20th-century house, set amid magnificent grounds complete with a pool, tennis court, and nature trail. Gourmet meals are available.

Abracadabra

MAP C2 ▪ **Alto do Humaita 13, Búzios** ▪ **(022) 2623 1217** ▪ **www.abracadabra pousada.com.br** ▪ **$$$**
This establishment offers the same enviable views out over Búzios and the Atlantic as its sister hotel, Casas Brancas, but the rooms are smaller and plainer, and the rates are cheaper. It is just five minutes from the bustling Rua das Pedras.

Casas Brancas

MAP C2 ▪ **Alto do Humaitá 8, Búzios** ▪ **(022) 2623 1458** ▪ **www.casas brancas.com.br** ▪ **$$$**
Búzios's plushest hotel comprises a series of mock-Moorish villas on the side of a hill overlooking the Atlantic and the Ilha Branca. The town center and the best of the restaurants and shops are a five-minute walk away, and beach buggies are available for hire. The hotel has all the usual services, along with an excellent spa, an infinity pool, and three atmospheric restaurants.

Pousada do Sandi

MAP A2 ▪ **Rua do Rosário 1, Paraty** ▪ **(024) 3371 2100** ▪ **www.pousada dosandi.com.br** ▪ **$$$**
The most comfortable and well appointed of all the *pousadas* in Paraty's colonial center has a spa, a good restaurant, and a bar serving *caipirinhas*.

Pousada Literária de Paraty

MAP A2 ▪ **Rua do Comércio 362, Paraty** ▪ **(024) 3371 8325** ▪ **www.hotelcoxixo.com.br** ▪ **$$$**
This hotel offers 11 luxuriously fitted rooms facing onto an outdoor pool. The two suites located on the upper floor are among some of the best rooms in town.

Pousada Picinguaba

MAP A3 ▪ **Rua G 130, Vila Picinguaba** ▪ **(11) 2495 1586** ▪ **www.picinguaba.com** ▪ **$$$**
Only an hour beyond Paraty, this gorgeous retreat has ten tastefully decorated rooms, or a three-bed villa, in the Serra do Mar forest reserve, one of the most beautiful and well-preserved stretches of Brazilian coastline. Activities include private schooner cruises, guided jungle treks, and snorkeling in the bay.

Sagu Mini-Resort

MAP A2 ▪ **Praia Brava, Abraão, Ilha Grande** ▪ **(024) 3361 5823** ▪ **www.saguresort.com** ▪ **$$$**
At this romantic island hideaway, nine rooms with balconies and surrounded by tropical gardens overlook Abraão Bay. Facilities include a restaurant, breakfast, kayaks, and a solar-heated hot tub.

Solar do Império

MAP B2 ▪ **Av Koeler 376, Petrópolis** ▪ **(024) 2103 3000** ▪ **www.solardo imperio.com.br** ▪ **$$$**
The most luxurious hotel in Petrópolis is housed in a classically furnished 19th-century mansion on the city's grandest avenue, within walking distance of the principal sights. The hotel facilities include air-conditioned rooms, an excellent restaurant, outdoor and indoor pool, and a spa.

For a key to hotel price categories see p112

General Index

Acknowledgments

Author

Alex Robinson is a writer and photographer based in the UK and Brazil. He has worked for DK, *New York Times*, *Departures*, *Sunday Times Travel*, *M*, *Marie Claire*, and *Nota Bene* among other publications and specializes in luxury travel, adventure, and Lusitanian culture and music. Find out more about him on www.alexrobinsonphotography.co.uk.

Additional contributor
Huw Hennessy

Publishing Director Georgina Dee

Publisher Vivien Antwi

Design Director Phil Ormerod

Editorial Michelle Crane, Freddie Marriage, Rachel Fox, Fíodhna Ní Ghríofa, Scarlett O'Hara, Sally Schafer, Avijit Sengupta, Christine Stroyan

Design Richard Czapnik, Marisa Renzullo

Picture Research Phoebe Lowndes, Susie Peachey, Ellen Root, Oran Tarjan

Cartography Jasneet Kaur Arora, Simonetta Giori, Suresh Kumar, Casper Morris, Reetu Pandey

DTP Jason Little, George Nimmo, Azeem Siddiqui, Joanna Stenlake

Production Nancy-Jane Maun

Factchecker Fernanda Drummond

Proofreader Alyson Silverwood

Indexer Kathryn O'Donoghue

Commissioned Photography
Jose Olimpio, Alex Robinson, Rough Guides/Roger d'Olivere Mapp

First edition created by Quadrum Solutions, India

Picture Credits

The publisher would like to thank the following for their kind permission to reproduce their photographs:
(**Key:** a-above; b-below/bottom; c-centre; f-far; l-left; r-right; t-top)

4Corners: Guido Cozzi 3tr, 102-3; Günter Gräfenhain 3tl, 62-3; SIME/Antonino Bartuccio 1, 2tr, 4t, 4cla, 4crb, 4b, 34-5, 58t, 88-9.

Agency O Globo: Monica Imbuzeiro 19crb, 61br.

akg-images: Album/Prisma 36t.

Alamy Images: Alexandra 52br; Arco Images/Therin-Weise 19bl; bilwissedition Ltd. & Co. KG 37tr; Laura Coelho 25cb; David Davis Photoproductions 22-3; Hemis.fr./Bertrand Gardel 83cr; © Ildi.Food 41tr; imageBROKER/Florian Kopp 44t; INTERFOTO 36cb; JTB Media Creation, Inc. 32-3c; Mountain Light/Galen Rowell 14-5c; Robert Harding World Imagery/Yadid Levy 57tr.

AWL Images: Alex Robinson 19tl.

Bridgeman Images: Dom Pedro II, also known as Magnanimous (Rio de Janeiro, 1831-Paris, 1889), Emperor of Brazil /De Agostini Picture Library 37bl.

Colecao Museu Nacional de Belas Artes/PHAN/MinC: Arrufos by Belmiro de Almeida photo by César Barreto 20cla; Le Manteau Rouge by Tarila do Amaral/www.tarsiladoamaral.com.br photo by Romulo Fialdini 21tl; Primeira Missa no Brasil by Vitor Meireles photo by Jaime Acioli 20clb.

Corbis: Guido Cozzi 18-9c; epa /Antonio Lacerda 59tr; Farrell Grehan 98bl; Yadid Levy 92bl; Dimitri Lundt 45tr; Alex Robinson 14cl, 54tl.

Dorling Kindersley: Carregadora de perfume by Victor Brecheret ©DACS, London 2015 10br; Colonização e Dependência by Clécio Penedo, Museu Hitstorico Nacional 26cla; Cafe by Candido Portinari © DACS, London 2015 21br; Mural by Candido Portinari in the Instituto Moreira Salles, Instituto Moreira Salles, Gavea ©DACS, London 2015 77t.

Dreamstime.com: Celso Diniz 11bl; Dabldy 59bl; Ekaterinabelova 43tr; Filipe Frazao 4clb, 40bl, 92t; Lazyllama 45cl; Renato Machado 7tr; Marchello74 11crb; Mypix 78t; Paura 6ca; Pixattitude 10clb; Celso Pupo Rodrigues 44bl; Vincentho 2tl, 8-9.

Getty Images: Brazil Photos 98t; Stuart Dee 43cl; Luiz Grillo 46cr; Richard l'Anson 4cra; LatinContent/Luciana Whitaker 61cl; Lonely Planet 53t; Mario Tama 60bc.

Guimas Restaurante/Daniella Cavalcanti Assessoria de Imprensa: 81b.

Hotel Fasano Rio de Janeiro: 51t.

Irajá Gastrô: Alexander Landau 75cr.

Museu Histórico Nacional: 11tr.

Tyba Photographic Agency: J R Couto 16-7cr.

Jacket
Front and spine – **4Corners:** Günter Gräfenhain.
Back – **Getty Images:** Michael Marquand.

Pull-out map cover
4Corners: Günter Gräfenhain.

All other images are: © Dorling Kindersley. For further information see www.dkimages.com.

Penguin Random House

Printed and bound in China

First American Edition, 2009
Published in the United States by
DK Publishing, 345 Hudson Street,
New York, New York 10014

Copyright 2009, 2016 © Dorling Kindersley Limited

A Penguin Random House Company

15 16 17 18 10 9 8 7 6 5 4 3 2 1

Reprinted with revisions 2011, 2013, 2016

Published in Great Britain by Dorling Kindersley Limited.

A catalog record for this book is available from the Library of Congress.

ISSN 1479-344X
ISBN 978-1-4654-4092-1

SPECIAL EDITIONS OF DK TRAVEL GUIDES

DK Travel Guides can be purchased in bulk quantities at discounted prices for use in promotions or as premiums. We are also able to offer special editions and personalized jackets, corporate imprints, and excerpts from all of our books, tailored specifically to meet your own needs.

To find out more, please contact:

in the US
specialsales@dk.com

in the UK
travelguides@uk.dk.com

in Canada
specialmarkets@dk.com

in Australia
penguincorporatesales@ penguinrandomhouse.com.au

*As a guide to abbreviations in visitor information blocks: **Adm** = admission charge; **Av** = Avenida; **Btwn** = between; **Dis. access** = disabled access; **s/n** = sem número ("no number" in street address).*

Phrase Book

In an Emergency

Help!	Socorro!	sookorroo
Stop!	Pare!	pahree
Call a doctor!	Chame um médico!	shamih oong mehjikoo
Call an ambulance!	Chame uma ambulância!	shamih ooma amboolans-ya
Where is the hospital?	Onde é o hospital?	ohnd-yeh oo oshpital
Police!	Polícia!	poolees-ya
Fire!	Fogo!	fohgoo
I've been robbed	Fui assaltado	fwee asaltadoo

Communication Essentials

Yes	Sim	seeng
No	Não	nowng
Hello	Olá	ohla
How are you?	Como vai?	kohmoo vi
Goodbye	Tchau	tshow
See you later	Até logo	ateh logoo
Excuse me	Com licença	kong lisaynsa
I'm sorry	Desculpe	dishkoolp
Thank you	Obrigado (if a man is speaking)/	obrigadoo/
	obrigada (if a woman is speaking)	obrigada
Good morning	Bom dia	bong jeea
Good afternoon	Boa tarde	boh-a tarj
Good night	Boa noite	boh-a noh-itsh
Pleased to meet you	Muito prazer	mweengtoo prazayr
I'm fine	Estou bem/ tudo bem	shtoh bayng/ toodoo bayng
What?	O que?	oo kay
When?	Quando?	kwandoo
How?	Como?	kohmoo
Why?	Por que?	poorkay

Useful Phrases

On the left/right	À esquerda/ direita	a-shkayrda/ jirayta
I don't understand	Não entendo	nowng ayntayndoo
Please speak slowly	Fale devagar por favor	falee jivagar poor favohr
What's your name?	Qual é seu nome?	kwal eh say-oo nohm
My name is…	Meu nome é…	may-oo nohm eh
Go away!	Vá embora!	va aymbora
That's fine	Está bem	shtah bayng
Where is…?	Onde está…?	ohnj shtah

Useful Words

big	grande	granj
small	pequeno	pikaynoo
hot	quente	kayntsh
cold	frio	free-oo
bad	mau	mow
good	bom	bong
open	aberto	abehrtoo
closed	fechado	fishadoo
dangerous	perigoso	pirigohzoo

safe	seguro	sigooroo
first floor	primeiro andar	primayroo andar
ground floor	térreo	tehrryoo
lift	elevador	elevadohr
toilet	banheiro	ban-yayroo
men's	dos homens	dooz ohmaynsh
women's	das mulheres	dash moolyerish
entrance	entrada	ayntrada
exit	saída	sa-eeda
passport	passaporte	pasaportsh

Post Offices and Banks

bank	banco	bankoo
bureau de change	(casa de) câmbio	(kaza jih) kamb-yoo
exchange rate	taxa de câmbio	tasha jih kamb-yoo
post office	correio	koorray-oo
postcard	cartão postal	kartowng pooshtal
postbox	caixa de correio	kisha jih koorray-oo
ATM	caixa automática	kisha owtoomatshika
stamp	selo	sayloo
cash	dinheiro	jeen-yayroo
withdraw money	tirar dinheiro	tshirar jeen-yayroo

Shopping

How much is it?	Quanto é?	kwantweh
I would like…	Eu quero…	ay-oo kehroo
clothes	roupa	rohpa
This one	Esta	ehshta
That one	Essa	ehsa
market	mercado	merkadoo
Do you accept credit cards?	Aceitam cartão de crédito?	asaytowng kartowng jih krehditoo
expensive	caro	karoo

Sightseeing

museum	museu	moozay-oo
art gallery	galeria de arte	galiree-a jih artsh
national park	parque nacional	parkee nas-yoonal
beach	praia	pri-a
river	rio	ree-oo
church	igreja	igray-Ja
cathedral	catedral	katidrow
district	bairro	birroo
garden	jardim	Jardeeng
tourist office	informações turísticas	infoormasoyngsh oreeshtsheekash
guide	guia	gee-a
ticket	bilhete/ ingresso	bil-yaytsh/ ingrehsoo

Transport

bus	ônibus	ohniboosh
boat	barco	barkoo
train	trem	trayng
airport	aeroporto	a-ayroopohrtoo
airplane	avião	av-yowng
flight	vôo	voh-oo
bus stop	ponto de ônibus	pohntoo j-yohniboosh

bus station	**rodoviária**	*roodohvyar-ya*
train station	**estação de trem**	*stasowng jih trayng*
ticket	**passagem**	*pasaJayng*
taxi	**táxi**	*taxee*
subway	**metrô**	*metroh*

Health

I feel bad/ill	**Sinto-me mal/ doente**	*seentoomih mow/dwayntsh*
I need to rest	**Preciso descansar**	*priseezoo jishkansar*
pharmacy	**farmácia**	*farmas-ya*
medicine	**remédio**	*rimehd-yoo*
sanitary towels/ tampons	**absorventes/ tampões**	*absoovayntsh/ tampoyngsh*
mosquito repellent	**repelente de mosquito**	*ripelayntsh dih mooshkeetoo*
doctor	**médico**	*mehjikoo*
condom	**camisinha**	*kamizeen-ya*

Staying in a Hotel

hotel	**hotel**	*ohteh-oo*
boutique hotel	**pousada**	*pohzada*
guesthouse	**pensão**	*paynsowng*
hostel	**albergue**	*owbehrgee*
Do you have a room?	**Tem um quarto?**	*tayng oong kwartoo*
I have a reservation	**Tenho uma reserva**	*tayn-yoo ooma risehrva*
single/double (room)	**(quarto de) solteiro/casal**	*(kwartoo jih) sooltayroo/ kazow*
towel	**toalha**	*twal-ya*
toilet paper	**papel higiênico**	*papel-oo iJ -yehnikoo*

Eating Out

I want to reserve a table	**Quero reservar uma mesa**	*kehroo rizirvar ooma meyza*
The bill, please	**A conta, por favor**	*a kohnta, poor favohv*
menu	**cardápio/ menu**	*kardap-yoo/ maynoo*
wine list	**lista de vinhos**	*leeshta de veen-yoosh*
glass	**copo**	*kopoo*
bottle	**garrafa**	*garrafa*
restaurant	**restaurante**	*rishtowrantsh*
breakfast	**café da manhã**	*kafeh da man-yang*
lunch	**almoço**	*owmohsoo*
dinner/supper	**jantar**	*Jantar*
(mineral) water	**água (mineral)**	*agwa (minerow)*
vegetarian	**vegetariano**	*vigitar-yanoo*
Is service included?	**O serviço está incluído?**	*oo sirveesoo shtah inklweedoo*

Menu Decoder

açúcar	*asookar*	sugar
alho	*al-yoo*	garlic
arroz	*arrohsh*	rice
azeite	*azaytsh*	olive oil
bebida	*bibeeda*	drink
bem passado	*bayng pasadoo*	well done
bife	*beefee*	steak

café	*kafeh*	coffee
cerveja	*sirvay.Ja*	beer
chá	*sha*	tea
churrasco	*shoorrashkoo*	barbecue
feijão (preto)	*fayJowng (praytoo)*	(black) beans
frango	*frangoo*	chicken
fruta	*froota*	fruit
lanche	*lanshee*	snack
leite	*laytsh*	milk
pão	*powng*	bread
pimenta	*pimaynta*	pepper
mal passado	*mow pasadoo*	rare
sal	*sow*	salt
vinho	*veen-yoo*	wine
ao ponto	*ow pohntoo*	medium
feijoada	*fayJwada*	bean and meat stew
sorvete	*sohrvaytsh*	ice cream
manteiga	*mantayga*	butter
grelhado	*gril-yadoo*	grilled
batatas fritas	*batatash freetash*	chips
carne	*karnee*	beef
peixe	*payshee*	fish

Time

minute	**minuto**	*minootoo*
hour	**hora**	*ora*
half an hour	**meia hora**	*may-a ora*
Monday	**segunda-feira**	*sigoonda fayra*
Tuesday	**terça-feira**	*tayrsa fayra*
Wednesday	**quarta-feira**	*kwarta fayra*
Thursday	**quinta-feira**	*keenta fayra*
Friday	**sexta-feira**	*sayshta fayra*
Saturday	**sábado**	*sabadoo*
Sunday	**domingo**	*doomeengoo*

Numbers

1	**um/uma**	*oong/ooma*
2	**dois/duas**	*doh-ish/doo-ash*
3	**três**	*traysh*
4	**quatro**	*kwatroo*
5	**cinco**	*seenkoo*
6	**seis**	*saysh*
7	**sete**	*seht*
8	**oito**	*oh-itoo*
9	**nove**	*novee*
10	**dez**	*dehsh*
11	**onze**	*ohnzee*
12	**doze**	*dohzee*
13	**treze**	*trayzee*
14	**catorze**	*katohrzee*
15	**quinze**	*keenzee*
16	**dezesseis**	*dizesaysh*
17	**dezessete**	*dizesehtee*
18	**dezoito**	*dizoh-itoo*
19	**dezenove**	*dizenovee*
20	**vinte**	*veentee*
30	**trinta**	*treenta*
40	**quarenta**	*kwaraynta*
50	**cinqüenta**	*sinkwaynta*
60	**sessenta**	*sesaynta*
70	**setenta**	*setaynta*
80	**oitenta**	*oh-itaynta*
90	**noventa**	*nohvaynta*
100	**cem, cento**	*sayng/sayntoo*

Selected Street Index